George A. Maloney, S.J.

IN JESUS WE TRUST

AVE MARIA PRESS
Notre Dame, Indiana 46556

248
ma I

ACKNOWLEDGMENTS

Sincere gratitude to Mary Louise Leonard for her generous efforts in typing this manuscript and for proofreading the text, and to Mrs. June Culver for her suggestions, which proved most helpful.

Unless otherwise noted, all scripture quotations are taken from THE JERUSA-LEM BIBLE, copyright ©1966 by Darton, Longman & Todd, Ltd. and Doubleday & Company, Inc. Used by permission of the publisher.

Imprimi Potest:
Rev. Patrick Burns, S.J.
Provincial of Wisconsin Province
of the Society of Jesus

International Standard Book Number: 0-87793-429-0
                                     0-87793-428-2 (pbk.)

Library of Congress Catalog Card Number: 90-82097

Cover and text design by Elizabeth J. French

Printed and bound in the United States of America.

To Hortense Bugbee and Ruggles Richmond,
who have learned trust the old-fashioned way.

Table of Contents

Introduction

The prophet Jeremiah, near the end of the seventh century B.C., commented on the world in which he was living in these words: "'Peace! Peace!' they say, but there is no peace. They should be ashamed of their abominable deeds. But not they!" (Jer 6:14-15). All of us, the world over, crave peace in our individual lives, in our families, in our cities and countries and in the entire universe. How pathetically all of us seek that inner rest and peace for which St. Augustine so desperately was searching when he wrote in his *Confessions*: "Thou hast made us for Thyself, O Lord, and our hearts are restless until they rest in Thee!"

All human beings are plagued by fears and anxieties about their past, as well as their future. Death confronts us with leering countenance and grasping tentacles that are always stretching out to snatch us into a dark world of meaninglessness.

When God's Word became man-among-us, he taught us to trust in the heavenly Father as he, Jesus, did. He gives us his Holy Spirit, who makes it possible to abandon ourselves to our loving Father. We are to put aside all nervous and excessive anxiety about temporal concerns and, by trusting in the providential care of our heavenly Father over all our needs, we will live in love and peace and joy through the Spirit.

Without Me You Can Do Nothing

What great wisdom for us to be penetrated by the Spirit's inner knowledge that we are totally weak of ourselves, but our strength is completely in God who truly loves us. As true children of God we realize in life's circumstances that we have no strength of our own. In all moments we must confess our weakness to do any good by ourselves. With St. Paul, we should believe that all our strength is in Christ.

True strength begins with a realization that of ourselves we are weak, but our very weakness confessed becomes our strength because we lovingly surrender to God in all things and expect God to come to our assistance: "...my power is at its best in weakness" (2 Co 12:9–10).

The sign of a true Christian consists in a constant, loving submission and obedience to God's commands and wishes. To believe that the Father truly loves us and does all things out of love is the basis for our childlike surrender.

> I need only say, "I am slipping,"
> and your love, Yahweh, immediately supports me;
> and in the middle of all my troubles
> you console me and make me happy (Ps 94:18–19).

Building Trust in God

I have tried in this book to present a theological basis for building our complete, childlike trust upon the Trinity, as found in God's revelation in scripture and the teaching of the church, especially in the writings of the great Christian contemplatives.

In order to ground ourselves in deep trust, I attempt in the opening chapter to lead the reader to discover that the reason we can truly trust in God is because God is *goodness*. He is more than the good works we trust he will do for us in our many needs. He *is* goodness!

God we know is love by his nature. But in God's relationships to us, he is love in action. And his actions must always be *good* since they flow from a triune community of divine love. God cannot do any action, except that he is love and goodness, and only loving and good actions can flow from his divine nature.

But God's greatest goodness is shown when his only-begotten Son took on our humanity and freely died for our happiness. Jesus Christ is the perfect image of the Trinity as he dies to reveal God's goodness in action (Chapter 2).

We prayerfully are led by Jesus in his evolving human consciousness to learn of him, "gentle and humble in heart" (Mt 11:28), how we, living in him, the risen-Lord, can trust in our Father, as Jesus did in his earthly life.

Why Are You So Anxious?

From the gospels Jesus teaches us how to be healed of the fears that destroy our peace by trusting absolutely in God's providential care in all details and needs of our lives (Chapter 3). Our God is "not far from any of us" (Acts 17:27), but through his uncreated energies of love he lovingly and actively is concerned about every detail of our life.

Possessing God's *shalom*, which Jesus brings to us through his teachings, his outpoured Holy Spirit, his intimate indwelling presence within us, we enter into an integration of all our God-given powers to bring them completely under obedience to the Father of us all through childlike trust. His perfect love drives out all fears. We begin to enjoy a harmony within ourselves since we are at one with the indwelling Trinity. We work to bring such harmony or tranquility of order to the world immediately around us.

Chapter 4 develops the theme of trust in God's forgiving love. Perhaps most Christians are in greatest need of trusting that God truly loves us and that in Christ's sacrifice of love unto death God truly has forgiven us our sins. What trust in God's love for us is required to believe in God's forgiving mercy that Jesus Christ, the Lamb of God, takes away all our sins!

The Sacrament of the Present Moment

Concretely, trust is developed only in the moment that confronts us *now*. The past is over. The future is far away and may never come into the present moment as we would desire. Our God is an incarnational God, found in each moment, in each particle of matter, working out of infinite love for us, his children.

Not only are we to trust that God is meeting us in each moment, but he is also humbly asking us to cooperate to make this a more beautiful universe, which will bring to completion his creation. We have the power to "enspirit" the matter of the universe into a unity of the total Christ (Chapter 5).

Trusting in Human Love

All of God's creation unveils his loving and self-sacrificing gift of himself to his children. Yet God most reveals his loving presence to each of us through the love we have for other human persons (Chapter 6).

> No one has ever seen God;
> but as long as we love one another

God will live in us
and his love will be complete in us (1 Jn 4:12).

What joys come to us as we not only encounter the uniqueness of the other person, but also God's loving, self-emptying in
that very love. Yet, what agonies and sufferings such human love
encounters and has to transform into greater trust of God and
the beloved.

God created us not to be alone, but to be completed by his
love through the pass-over experience needed to discover one's
uniqueness in living in love for another. But to answer God's call
to love others as Jesus has loved us is to be ready to suffer to build
the necessary trust that precedes true, agapic love of God and
the beloved.

Trusting in Time of Suffering

Chapter 7 tries to confront the perennial question all human
beings ask of God and of each other: Why must human beings,
especially the young and innocent, suffer so unjustly before great
evils in our world if God is supposed to be *love* and omnipotent?
An adequate, rational answer to the problem of suffering and evil
in this world can never be given. Christianity, however, through
the Spirit's infusion of faith, hope and love, and the teachings and
example of Jesus, points to a knowledge that leads us beyond any
human understanding into the world of mystery. In this world,
like Job, we learn to trust in God's omnipotence and perfect love
for us, his children, that operate in each event, even if we do not
rationally understand the *how*.

St. Paul directs us to the only Way to trust in sufferings:

We know that by turning everything to their good God
co-operates with all those who love him, with all those
that he has called according to his purpose. They are the
ones he chose specially long ago and intended to become
true images of his Son (Rom 8:28–29).

Trust in the Dark Night

Chapter 8 serves to summarize this entire book on trust by
focusing upon the most intense purifications that God sends or
permits to happen to those who have advanced in their lives and

in their accompanying prayer to a mystical, transforming union with Jesus Christ, the Bridegroom, through the heavenly Father in the Holy Spirit.

In the intense sufferings of an active and passive nature such as the great mystics have undergone, we seek to bring together the relationship between sufferings and the development of trusting abandonment to the indwelling Trinity. Such surrendering through the Spirit to Christ brings about a transformation to oneness as we die to all self-centeredness and live only for him.

A childlike trust that transforms our will into the one will of God allows God to work through us to the degree that we surrender to Christ. In oneness with Christ we can in faith, trust and love, work with Christ to build his body, the church. It is in Jesus we trust!

George A. Maloney, S.J.

CHAPTER 1

God Is Goodness

You and I are very lonely hunters. We stalk through the jungles of our cities and mountains seeking love and happiness. All of us desperately desire to love someone beautiful and to be loved ardently by someone who is good. We move through life toward love with unrelentling striving, more so than any wild animal seeking food or drink.

But, alas, like little children who gleefully stretch out to grasp the brilliantly shining soap bubbles that dance so enticingly away from them, we too grasp our own bubbles that dissolve, leaving us with a handful of emptiness. God has created us to seek out the good and the beautiful and to find ourselves in relationships to other knowing and loving beings. Through such love relationships we are to discover the loving beauty of God and to know in our heart that he is the supreme goodness from whom comes all finite, participated good.

In surrendering to another, and ultimately to God in unselfish love, we reach the highest state of communication that leads to communion. In such intimate self-giving communion we expand into a conscious awareness of being one in a mutual sharing of the good within both the lover and the beloved, while at the same time we both discover how beautifully unique and free we are to live in goodness toward the other.

Love — A Call to Suffer

Yet we know from our limited experiences in loving relationships both with other human beings and with God that our *I-ness* can never be static. We long to be more ourselves in a dynamic process of believing in the other and having faith in our goodness, of trusting in the other, that alone leads to greater loving union.

Experiencing the sense of identity in love through an expanded consciousness that grows in intensity, we not only want more of the same awareness, but we cannot live without it. In a way we can say that love is a call to suffer, for it means that all

lesser desires — above all, any egocentrism — must be put to
death. We cannot live now except to love more. But to love
more, we must move away from our own self-control and, in
humble trust in the goodness of the other, learn to surrender.

Not to love, once we have experienced a beautiful love, is to
tear our true self into shreds. It is to deny the goodness of the
other, as well as our own goodness in losing such love. This is why
separation is so painful when a deep level of unity in love has been
reached by two persons. This is also why it should be so death-
dealing for us human beings, in selfishness and illusory independence, to walk away from God, the source of all good, who is
goodness itself.

Made to God

St. Augustine realized what all of us should acknowledge
experientially at some time or other in our lifetime, as he wrote in
his *Confessions*: "Thou hast made us for Thyself, O Lord, and our
hearts are restless until they rest in Thee!" We are superior to
animals and all other material creatures insofar as we possess
spiritual faculties of intellect and will in order to know God as
the source of all beauty and good and to love him as the sole
possessor of all goodness. We have been made by God to seek with
unending appetite whatever is good and beautiful. Our human
will cannot move to possess anything that it would recognize as
evil. We willingly seek out only what is presented by our intellect
as good.

The thirst of our intellect is expressed in the words of the
psalmist: "Who will give us sight of happiness?" (Ps 4:6). Since by
our faith God is the absolute good, and all that he does is good, we
should all desire to be united with perfect Goodness. Stretching
out to touch and love the good in any human being leaves us
always in an existential pain of incompleteness, of more emptiness than infilling.

God is above all the finite limitations and imperfections of his
creatures. Creatures are but participated goods, reflecting a weak
spark of God's flaming beauty and perfection. We creatures are
mere drops of his goodness. God is a teeming, unbounded ocean of
goodness, which can fill the largest, as well as the smallest, of
rivulets or streams.

He contains in himself the sweetness of all other goods. Creatures are uncertain goods, but not goodness in their very beings. They begin to exist. They also may cease to be. Here today, gone tomorrow. All limited perfections that draw us to desire a share in the goods of creatures cry out to us that they can never completely satisfy the longing in our hearts for the perfect, unlimited beauty that is God himself. Several creatures answer different needs we have, but only God can answer all our desires.

This is why God implants within our hearts a spark of desire that can be fanned into a blazing flame if we only seek him passionately as the supreme beauty and goodness in our lives.

With the psalmist we can confess:

> God, you are my God, I am seeking you,
> my soul is thirsting for you,...
> a land parched, weary and waterless;
> I long to gaze on you in the Sanctuary,
> and to see your power and glory.

> Your love is better than life itself,
> my lips will recite your praise;
> all my life I will bless you,
> in your name lift up my hands;...

> for you have always helped me.
> I sing for joy in the shadow of your wings;
> my soul clings close to you,
> your right hand supports me (Ps 63:1–8).

At the heart of being truly human is this spiritual thirst for God as our ultimate good. We can thrill in viewing a beautiful sunset or in hearing a Beethoven or Mozart symphony. We can experience in deep love the unique goodness and beauty of another person. And yet, there will always be some pull of pain that such complexity in unified harmony cannot always last for us and cannot be infinite, experienced all the time, ever increasing. God has made us to stretch out to make contact with the Absolute Being, to possess the Unpossessible, who makes all other possessions vain.

> As a doe longs
>> for running streams,
> so longs my soul
>> for you, my God.
>
> My soul thirsts for God,
>> the God of life;
> when shall I go to see
>> the face of God? ...
>
> Deep is calling to deep
>> as your cataracts roar;
> all your waves, your breakers,
>> have rolled over me.
>
> In the daytime may Yahweh
>> command his love to come,
> and by night may his song be on my lips,
>> a prayer to the God of my life!
>
> Let me say to God my Rock,
>> "Why do you forget me?" ...
>
> Put your hope in God: I shall praise him yet,
>> my savior, my God (Ps 42:1–2,7–9,11).

Only God Is Good

We can believe in God, our Father, who creates all things in heaven and earth. We can believe in some way that God is good because he pours out his gifts of good things that we need for our physical, psychical and spiritual growth. All the beautiful creatures that God gives to us cry out as signposts pointing to our great Benefactor. The variety of beauty in his many gifts, the richness, the plentitude that we have all received leave us breathless before God's generosity.

St. Augustine movingly writes:

> Heaven and earth and all that is in the universe cry out to me from all directions that I, O God, must love Thee, and they do not cease to cry out to all so that they have no excuse.

But God is more than a good giver of gifts. He is good by his very nature. "God is love" (1 Jn 4:8). But for God to be love by his very nature means that he is always loving. To love is to live for the goodness and happiness of one another. Therefore, love and goodness in God are the same. God is love and goodness by his very nature. God could not be now good, then evil, and still be God. The essence of God is to be always loving goodness.

Jesus gives us a teaching that flows out of the constant belief in Judaism that rightly held that God alone is good. In Mark's gospel we find the rich young man running with enthusiasm to Jesus and kneeling before him as he asks what more should he still do to enter into the kingdom of heaven. He addresses Jesus as "good master," to which greeting Jesus responds: "Why do you call me good? No one is good but God alone" (Mk 10:18).

Some commentators think Jesus was drawing the young man of great wealth to a deeper faith and trust in him than one would give an ordinary man. Goodness for the Jews is a title due only to God. Could Jesus be asking the young man whom he looked upon with love (Mk 10:21) to a decision to declare Jesus as more than a mere human being? "If you account me good, then account me God and not merely a human person." At least we are sure that Jesus was asking him to sell all his possessions, give them to the poor and, placing all his trust in Jesus and his goodness, to follow him. The decision was too much of a sacrifice in faith and trust in Jesus as truly good and divine; the rich young man's "face fell at these words and he went away sad, for he was a man of great wealth" (Mk 10:22).

Jesus asserts that only God is goodness. God is good of himself. All created good is a mere reflection of God's perfect goodness. He is the absolute good, the source of all participated good. God depends on no other for his goodness. If we human beings or any other creatures possess any goodness or any perfection, it is a sharing in the breath of God's own goodness upon them. St. James writes in his epistle: "It is all that is good, everything that is perfect, which is given us from above; it comes down from the Father of all light; with him there is no such thing as alteration, no shadow of a change" (Jas 1:17).

Goodness Is Loving Sharing

God is goodness by his very nature. He needs no other outside of his God-head nature to make him good. And all other creatures are good because he shares with them a participation in his goodness. In him there is only goodness and from him only goodness can proceed.

We will now show how Jesus Christ, God's Word made flesh and come among us, is God's greatest, manifested goodness to us. Being so good in himself, God so loved us and his created world as to give us his only-begotten Son that we might have a share in his goodness. If God is love and goodness by his very being, then he is always seeking by his nature to share his goodness by means of communicating his presence to us.

Creating us according to God's image and likeness is a free choice on God's part that we might share in his goodness. God becomes a God-toward-us in his perfect goodness by communicating himself to us through his Word in his Spirit of love. God creates the whole world as good to show his burning desire to give himself in faithful communication through his Word.

Although God is first and always goodness in sharing between the Father and the Son in the mutual binding of goodness and love (the Holy Spirit), nevertheless, only through God's gift of the Word made flesh can we come to know God's goodness as sharing within the community of the Trinity.

God's fullest revelation as love and goodness by nature is made in his incarnate Word, Jesus Christ. For in him we have not only words, but we have the one Word that is the perfect copy of God's nature. In him we can come not only to know God's very nature as a community of mutual, sharing persons, Father, Son and Holy Spirit, but we can be brought into a loving communion with God's very being through the risen Lord's Spirit. We can become good, not in ourselves, but as true participators in God's very own nature.

Knowing the Word Incarnate in scripture and church teaching, we can now know the Father and his Spirit through whom the Word makes the Father known. We, by listening to the Word enfleshed for love of us, can know what the inner life of the Trinity is like. If God is goodness by nature, and goodness is communicative and diffusive, we can infallibly participate in God's goodness as expressed in the communitarian sharing within the Trinity.

The Trinity is the model of the same energies of love that are shared with us, who are outside of that essential life of the triune God, who no human being can ever see and live.

Goodness Within the Trinity

God is not a monotheistic, absolute being, existing as one person in self-contained "goodness." Goodness, as we have said, is always "toward" others in a self-emptying love that seeks to share personhood. In so being "othered," each person is unique. God in his essence is a community of love, of self-giving persons in perfect unity of mutual goodness. Yet, in the unique relationships of Father, Son and Holy Spirit, the Trinity brings about the possibility of unique self-giving.

In absolute silence, in a communication of love and goodness impossible for human beings to understand, God the Father, the "unoriginated source of being," speaks his one eternal Word through his Spirit of love. In that one Word the Father is perfectly present, totally self-giving to his Son. "In his body lives the fullness of divinity" (Col 2:9).

In his Spirit the Father also hears his Word come back to him in a perfect, eternal yes of total surrendering love that is again the Holy Spirit. The Trinity is a reciprocal community, a movement of perfect goodness, measured by total self-emptying as free gift in love to the Other. Our weak minds cannot fathom the peace and joy, the ardent excitement and exuberant self-surrender that flow in reposeful motion between Father and Son through the Holy Spirit. God is really God because in utter goodness he can communicate in Love with his Word.

God's Shared Goodness Through Creation

God is always loving and good in all relationships. Revelation assures us that the Father freely creates a world of dependent creatures out of the perfect goodness experienced with the other two Persons in the trinitarian family — all in order that we might share somewhat in God's goodness. In wishing to share with others outside of the perfect, trinitarian community of love, God could never be motivated to create out of a lack of goodness. Creation can only be explained as a manifestation of God's goodness. God freely creates out of absolute goodness, not out of a deprivation of some good, in order that nothingness can be something, or someone, that participates in God's very own goodness.

Tied to the mysterious makeup of God as an *I* that is also a *We*, is God's bursting forth from within his own perfect, circular, loving, good self-containment to love us and share with us his goodness. The nature of God is to be good. But goodness is intrinsically ordered toward communication and sharing in intimate communion with others. God in his goodness spills out his love in activities that must be always good since they freely come out of a good God. God would cease to be God if any of his actions were anything less than a manifestation of the perfect goodness intrinsic to God's very own nature.

This is why scripture attests that God creates his creatures as participators of his own goodness and, therefore, all of creation is good. "God saw all he had made, and indeed it was very good" (Gn 1:31). "Everything God has created is good" (1 Tm 4:4), affirms St. Paul. All creatures have some participation in God's goodness. They reflect a spark of God's infinite beauty and goodness. God loves that goodness in creation; otherwise, he would not love himself as the source of all goodness. God cannot hate any of his creatures, including devils.

An enemy is one who wishes evil to another. God cannot absolutely wish evil to the damned. God's justice by way of punishment inflicted upon his creatures must always be a part of his goodness.

God's goodness is his most beautiful and sweet perfection. It is not one of his many attributes. It is his very essence. He cannot be what he is, the absolute God, without also being goodness by nature. We will see that we come to trust in him in all his works toward us because all such acts flow from his very nature as goodness. We stand in amazement of God's omnipotent power. This knowledge comes to us through our understanding of cause and effect. We understand God's wisdom in ordering all things harmoniously, and this astonishes us unceasingly. But God as good and bountiful is an object of our will that brings forth love and desire.

Moses wanted to see God's glory, but God responded to his request: "I will let all my splendor pass in front of you, and I will pronounce before you the name Yahweh. I have compassion on whom I will, and I show pity to whom I please" (Ex 33:19). Then, Yahweh promises Moses that he will see something of his glory pass by:

> Here is a place beside me. You must stand on the rock, and when my glory passes by, I will put you in a cleft of the rock and shield you with my hand while I pass by. Then I will take my hand away and you shall see the back of me; but my face is not to be seen (Ex 33:21–23).

God's Goodness in Matter

We see God's reflected goodness in his ongoing creation, redemption and providence in guiding all of creation to its intended goal. Creation is the first act of God's goodness outside of the Trinity. It is not primarily a work of mercy, which has as its object a miserable and sinful creation toward which God shows compassion and forgiveness. The most basic act in wishing to create is to materialize his love and goodness. The whole world is a map to represent and a mirror to reflect his goodness. "Yahweh's tenderness embraces all his creatures" (Ps 145:9). He is manifested as good *in* all.

Especially is God good in the very creation of man and woman according to his very own image and likeness.

> Ah, what is man that you should spare a thought for him,
> the son of man that you should care for him?
> Yet you have made him little less than a god,
> you have crowned him with glory and splendor,
> made him lord over the work of your hands,
> set all things under his feet (Ps 8:4–6).

Self-Gift of God to Man and Woman

The millions of creatures that constantly tumble forth from God's fingertips can never adequately image God's tremendous passion to communicate himself to us more perfectly. God's Word

spoken in all of creation is only a means by which this outpouring
God can be more intimately present in beautiful goodness to one
unique creation — man and woman.

In the book of Genesis God is depicted as a self-communicat-
ing community, freely deciding on a new course of creative living.

> God said, "Let us make man in our own image, in the
> likeness of ourselves, and let them be masters of the fish of
> the sea, the birds of heaven, the cattle, all the wild beasts
> and all the reptiles that crawl upon the earth."
>
> God created man in the image of himself,
> in the image of God he created him,
> male and female he created them (Gn 1:26-37).

God creates man and woman in such a way that in this very
process man and woman are summoned to receive the Word
actively, that is, they are called to listen, to understand and to
believe in God's goodness as communicated to them. God creates
them in such a way that they know they are determined and
conditioned by God's goodness and, by freely accepting him as
the source of all their gifts and beauty, in loving trust and
obedience, they too can be transformed into good and beautiful
children of God. The index of how freely they accept God's
goodness and are transformed by him is seen in their human
response to God's call to be holy and good as he is.

Man and woman alone among all God's creatures are able to
know God's goodness and by a willing, free choice can respond by
means of a decision. The true dignity of human beings consists in
being created by God in order to be able to reply to him. Only in
this answer do they fulfill the purpose of God's creation. The first
man and woman walked with God and dialogued with him in the
cool of the day: a picture of peace and repose (Gn 2:8,15). But
before that familiarity could flower into a community of shared
life, sin entered.

Sin — An Absence of God's Goodness

Sin is an act whereby man and woman close their spiritual
ears to God's Word. They no longer want to be present to God's
loving presence. Although we human beings cannot prevent God

from being actively good in all his actions as a loving presence in our lives, we can run from that presence, thinking we can hide and reject his goodness.

Because of sin Adam and his children begin their long pilgrimage in exile from God, who is ever present as goodness to them as he continually speaks his powerful, active, loving Word. God continues to be present, touching his human children in millions of ways, yet they freely continue to be blinded to his goodness in their lives.

God Is Good in His Covenant

God's goodness is shown by his pursuing love in establishing a covenant with his human children. He freely chooses one man, Abraham, to be the father of his people. The only condition for receiving God's continuous favors is that Abraham trust in God's protection and act in the belief that what is impossible to him is possible to God.

> Bear yourself blameless in my presence, and I will make a Covenant between myself and you, and increase your numbers greatly. ... Here now is my covenant with you: you shall become the father of a multitude of nations....
> I will make you most fruitful.... I will establish my Covenant between myself and you, and your descendants after you, generation after generation, a Covenant in perpetuity, to be your God and the God of your descendants after you. I will give to you and to your descendants after you the land you are living in, the whole land of Canaan, to own in perpetuity, and I will be your God (Gn 17:1–8).

He restores his covenant through Jacob and his children and also through his servant, repentant sinner, king and prophet, David. He speaks to his people through the goodness of his wisdom revealed to his prophets on behalf of his people. He lovingly brings his people back from exile and rebuilds their temple for them. The House of God sanctifies Jerusalem and makes her impregnable to all enemies. God's presence as communicating his Word was felt powerfully in that holy dwelling place.

God's Godness in His Word Made Flesh

But the absolute peak of God's goodness revealed to humanity is found in the summary of God's nature as goodness toward his creatures, when, in the succinct but pregnant words of his prologue John the Evangelist writes:

> The Word was made flesh,
> he lived among us,
> and we saw his glory,
> the glory that is his as the only Son of the Father,
> full of grace and truth (Jn 1:14).

St. Luke announces this tremendous incarnation of God's goodness to humanity through the announcement of singing angels who praise God for his goodness: "Glory to God in the highest heaven, and peace to [all] who enjoy his favor" (Lk 2:14).

When men and women fell from God's infinite goodness, he showed that he could never fall away from manifesting his infinite goodness to them. The greatest evil could not stop his wisdom from pouring out his goodness in even richer ways. St. Augustine called the very fall of men and women away from God a *"felix culpa,"* a "fortuitous failing," which received mercy and forgiveness in the most unmerited way in the form of God's only-begotten Son. Not only would Jesus Christ, the eternal Word of God within the Trinity, take upon himself our humanity and suffer temptations as all of us do, but he would freely image the great outpoured goodness of the heavenly Father by laying down his very own life on our behalf.

> Christ Jesus:
> was divine,
> yet he did not cling
> to his equality with God
> but emptied himself
> to assume the condition of a slave,
> and became as men are;
> and being as all men are,
> he was humbler yet,
> even to accepting death,
> death on a cross.

> But God raised him high
> and gave him the name
> which is above all other names
> so that *all beings*
> in the heavens, on earth and in the underworld,
> *should bend the knee* at the name of Jesus
> and that every tongue should acclaim
> Jesus Christ as Lord,
> to the glory of God the Father (Phil 2:6–11).

What more could be said about God's goodness toward us human beings than what St. Irenaeus in the second century wrote and what was repeated by St. Athanasius and so many of the early Fathers: "God became man, in order that man might become God!"? Not only did God's goodness in Jesus Christ take away our sins, but in a new and marvelous way it divinized us to become truly children of God,

> But to all who did accept him
> he gave power to become children of God,
> to all who believe in the name of him
> who was born not out of human stock
> or urge of the flesh
> or will of man
> but of God himself (Jn 1:12–13).

In creation God formed innocent creatures out of the earth. In redemption God restores our rebellious nature by the blood of his Son. St. Paul writes: "Remember how generous the Lord Jesus was: he was rich, but he became poor for your sake, to make you rich out of his poverty" (2 Cor 8:9).

And how truly enriched we have become through God's goodness revealed in Jesus Christ! God truly looks as Jesus looks; God loves us and shows infinite goodness and mercy to us in Jesus who dies out of sheer goodness on our behalf!

True Goodness Embraces the Cross

God's goodness cost a price beyond anything we could ever imagine. The price to reveal his goodness to us, his sinful children, who could never demand or claim in justice any such revelation, was not paid in any gold or treasures that belonged to

God as Creator of all things. It came out of the inner community of love, the Trinity, as this divine family dug inside itself and offered from within God the Word as the complete and perfect expression for all eternity of how truly good God is to us!

"Eternity" freely chooses to die that you and I may live eternally and share the triune divine life. The Lord of the universe and of angels freely weeps in a stable-cradle that we might rejoice forever. He hangs as a slave and criminal on a cross, poured out to the last drop of blood and water, that we might be exalted and share in his glory with the Father.

Goodness Invites Trust

As we ponder the personal sacrifices of Jesus Christ, can we ever forget his humble goodness shown to us? Can we ever be lacking in childlike trust and complete abandonment to a God who dies for us? This goodness is encountered still in the sacraments, the peak of which is the Eucharist. Here we daily are privileged to enter into the Trinity through the pierced heart of Jesus as he, yesterday, today and always, images in his sacrifice on the cross unto death for us and in the sacrament of his perfect love the goodness of our Father through his Son in his Spirit. As we take and eat his body and drink his blood unto the remission of our sins, we become aware, through the knowledge given us by the Spirit of the risen Savior, how perfect is God's goodness to us.

> The blessing-cup that we bless is a communion with the blood of Christ, and the bread that we break is a communion with the body of Christ (1 Cor 10:16).

The rest of this book will continually come back to this basic element of God as goodness by his very nature, manifesting in his uncreated energies the triune community's love in concrete actions of goodness. It is because of this that we can rejoice always and trust in God's loving activities in each human event as it happens to us. We can believe with St. Paul:

> We know that by turning everything to their good God co-operates with all those who love him, with all those that he has called according to his purpose. They are the ones he chose specially long ago and intended to become

true images of his Son, so that his Son might be the eldest of many brothers. He called those he intended for this; those he called he justified, and with those he justified he shared his glory.

After saying this, what can we add? With God on our side who can be against us? Since God did not spare his own Son, but gave him up to benefit us all, we may be certain, after such a gift, that he will not refuse anything he can give.... Nothing therefore can come between us and the love of Christ, even if we are troubled or worried, or being persecuted, or lacking food or clothes, or being threatened or even attacked.... These are the trials through which we triumph, by the power of him who loved us.

For I am certain of this: neither death nor life, no angel, no prince, nothing that exists, nothing still to come, not any power, or height or depth, nor any created thing, can ever come between us and the love of God made visible in Christ Jesus our Lord (Rom 8:28–39).

CHAPTER 2

Jesus Trusts in His Father

We have seen that God does not merely do good acts and give us good things for our happy fulfillment. He is *goodness!* In every divine thought and word communicated to us, and in every divine action, God is always good. He can never be evil or do any evil. He can never cease acting out of his nature as good. And, therefore, we can logically trust in him, who always seeks the best for us.

And yet, why do you and I not always trust absolutely in God's goodness and love in the concrete situations in which we find ourselves? In our limited experiences we are aware that our potential to return love is measured by the degree of love received and consciously experienced by us. God loves us infinitely and always acts out of his natural goodness toward us. The trouble lies in our lack of experiencing God's love through the gifts of the Holy Spirit — deep faith, hope and love for God.

The first movement for us to be loving is to receive self-sacrificing love. Are not the juvenile delinquents on our streets or in our correction institutions proof that we are shaped by the love we received or lacked in our lives? Loving people call us into a transcendence of selfgiving in return. With no love received, we resort to violence. We shout out in defiance to the world around us that we deserve to be loved, that we possess an inner beauty and a God-sharing goodness.

Jesus Christ: God's Goodness Enfleshed

We have seen that in God's plan to manifest his divine nature as goodness, he gives us his only-begotten Son, Jesus Christ, as the culmination and most perfect expression in human form of how great God's goodness and love are toward us.

William of St. Thierry gives us an important nuance of what constitutes a *person* through true love relationships. He coins the word *insinuatio* in Latin to describe that the Son and the Father are two lovers; they take each other to their breasts (*in sinu*

meaning in the bosom of) in an embrace (cf. Jn 1:18). They give
themselves to each other, and they allow each other to know
their identity in that mutual "uncovering."

Jesus knows the mind of the Father and reveals it to all who
open to his revelation. Jesus finds his whole *person* as the eternal
Word of God in being the total narration, unconcealment and
manifestation of his Father. To know Jesus is to know the Father.
Their mutual embrace, interpenetration and unconcealment are
so one through love for each other that one cannot be separated
from the other.

William expresses this beautifully:

> In effect, no one has ever seen God with these bodily
> eyes; but since the only Son is the very insinuation of the
> Father (*in sinu Patris*), and thereby uncovers the Father in
> an unspeakable telling, the purified and holy rational
> creature is permeated with this inexpressible vision. The
> creature is able to understand the Speaker narrating
> because He is *logos* — not the kind of word that strikes the
> ear as sound, but rather something like an imago (image)
> disclosed to the spirit. By an interior and manifest light,
> this telling clarifies the words of the Lord: "Philip, who-
> ever sees me sees the Father too" (*Against Peter Abelard*).

Jesus Had to Learn to Trust the Father

As God's eternal Word, the only-begotten Son received the
fullness of divinity from the Father and through the Spirit eternally surrendered himself back as perfect gift of love to the Father.
If Jesus came among us to teach us only about the goodness of
God, even by dying for us, we still would not understand how
humanly we should respond by trusting in God's goodness in all
our experiences.

Jesus is "the Way, the Truth and the Life" (Jn 14:6) whereby
we can experience God's perfect goodness toward us and, therefore, learn to trust in all of God's activities. Yet, Jesus is also in
human form the way we are to learn how to live in trust of the
heavenly Father in all details of our lives. No human consciousness ever grew progressively in experiencing the love from his
heavenly Father as did Jesus. At every moment he pushed himself

to new levels of awareness of this perfect love pouring into him out of the perfect goodness of his Father. His response was a childlike abandonment to surrender himself in a similar love returned.

St. Luke tells us: "And Jesus increased in wisdom, in stature, and in favor with God and men" (Lk 2:52). He grew progressively in trusting the Father in each human situation. As he experienced the Father's active, loving care for himself, Jesus learned experientially how to trust more completely in his self-surrender to the Father.

Jesus asked us to imitate him. "Shoulder my yoke and learn from me, for I am gentle and humble in heart" (Mt 11:29). Jesus learned to trust in his Father before he could ask us to imitate him. In this his humanity is more than a human reflection of the Father's goodness. Jesus shows what is available to us and how we too are to learn to trust in the same Father whom Jesus taught us to call our Father.

The Hidden Life

Jesus was conscious that everything he did came from his Father. This he had first to learn in the 30 hidden years he lived in Nazareth. He served the Father by seeking only to do his holy will and not his own. Jesus was a humble servant, seeking always to serve his Father whom he progressively learned to love in self-emptying love.

"The Son can do nothing by himself; he can do only what he sees the Father doing: and whatever the Father does the Son does too" (Jn 5:19). Jesus had to learn to live humanly with his own divinity. He had to discover in every facet of his humanity the presence of God working out of his perfect and infinite love and goodness and to yield that part of his being in loving trust and obedience to his Father.

He had to let go and learn to let God be the center of his life as he tempered his human will and intellect to the divine power that was at work in his unfolding human consciousness. It would be his human hands that would touch a leper and heal him. This experience of using his hands in loving touch was an experience he had to learn as he moved freely in surrendering trust to the power of his Father.

At Nazareth Jesus had to grow into a fully realized human personality that would be totally human, yet totally submissive in trust to the divine Father whom he progressively experienced in his humanity as dwelling intimately within him, making him and the Father one (Jn 17:21). He left Nazareth when he was ready. Tradition tells us it was about his 30th year of life. And yet, in his public life of preaching, healing and performing miracles, and above all in his temptations and sufferings leading to his death on the cross, he progressively continued to grow in greater self-surrender and perfect trust in the Father.

The End of Life

Jesus teaches us at Nazareth and during his remaining years of public service that the end of our lives, like the end of his human existence, is to move freely according to the inspirations of the Holy Spirit, who dwells within us and makes us aware of the perfect love of God for us. "The love of God has been poured into our hearts by the Holy Spirit which has been given us" (Rom 5:5). It is, as Jesus shows us, to bring ourselves completely through the Spirit into obedient abandonment to do always the will of the heavenly Father. It is, as Jesus did, to structure and discipline our bodies, souls and spirit relationships so as to move with authentic directness in the power of the Spirit through the Son to the Father.

This can be expressed briefly as familiarity with God. The Greek Fathers called it *parrhesia*, which they believed contained all other virtues and could be best described as a humble, childlike trust in God. Jesus in his humanity acquired this childlike trust first during the long, monotonous years at Nazareth.

Jesus moved his human consciousness and all his human powers directly through the indwelling Spirit to total oneness with the Father as he strove at each moment to give himself in complete self-surrender to the Father. In his life and ours this means the ability to find God easily in all things. It means sensitivity to his loving presence. It means a contentment in abiding in the Father's loving care, omnipotence, omniscience and omnipresence.

It means straightness and truth in the movement of Jesus' and our intentions to please God in every thought, word and deed. It means to allow ourselves willingly, as Jesus did, to be caught up in the total current of God's powerful love flowing strongly, yet gently throughout our life. It means that we learn from Jesus to have "interior eyes" to see, as he did, how all events, even those the world may label insignificant or unpleasant, can become exciting, creative points of unveiling the loving presence of God, who is always working to make all of us greater participators in God's own divine nature.

A Slow and Painful Growth

Jesus shows us that his growth took place slowly and in an unspectacular way as must our own individual growth in trusting God. Jesus first had to trust the Father working within the context of his very poor and simple life in Nazareth. Besides having only the bare necessities of life, the poverty of Jesus was a psychic and spiritual poverty. Jesus in his humanity experienced daily at Nazareth and throughout his earthly life that he was most radically and ontologically *non-being*, except for God's outpoured love in his unselfish giving of all that Jesus humanly possessed.

His poverty became, for Jesus, a humble recognition of God's sovereignty and free gift of his love. It is a permanent attitude of mind that Jesus assumed toward himself, his Father, and each person he met. It is a poverty that can be called humility. Jesus is nothing in his human creation. The Father is all. His Son is truly meek and humble of heart. He surrenders himself to do whatever the Father wishes him to do, both at Nazareth and on the cross: "Let your will be done, not mine" (Lk 22:42).

Jesus developed trust in his life of hard work, in his fatigue and sufferings. He had to labor hard and for long hours to earn the simple things he and his family needed to sustain them in life. His life was one continuous round of monotonous duties with little human satisfaction that his life was "going" anywhere. It was the interior spirit he had to develop to trust that, even in such banality and boredom, fatigue and little recompense, his life was giving glory and praise to God and was, therefore, truly worthwhile.

"Although he was Son, he learned to obey through suffering; but having been made perfect, he became for all who obey him the source of eternal salvation" (Heb 5:8–9). In the depths of his heart, his innermost consciousness, Jesus touched the holy presence of his Father. He breathed, smiled, laughed and cried in that holy presence of his infinitely loving Father. All outside creatures, touching Jesus in new, surprising experiences, were received as gifts by that delicate, sensitive, trusting gentleness in him.

When Jesus gave himself up to obey others, it was a joyful act of freedom to take his life in his hands and return it totally and freely back to his Father, source of all his being. Seeking only to do his Father's will, Jesus was able to obey others because he sought only to obey his Father.

Jesus Learned Trust in Prayer

Trust ultimately is measured by the degree of self-sacrifice and surrender one is able to give to the one trusted. It is in Jesus' deep encounters with the heavenly Father, living with his Spirit at the center of Jesus' consciousness, that he learned how to trust in the Father's goodness and love in his active life. Jesus lived what he taught his disciples: "when you pray, *go to your private room and, when you have shut the door, pray* to your Father who is in that secret place, and your Father who sees all that is done in secret will reward you" (Mt 6:6).

When Jesus spoke in Aramaic about prayer, he used the words *zla* and *zlotha*. Prayer in this sense means to tune in to the wavelength of God. Jesus prayed in the sense of always walking in the communicating presence of his Father. He sought to bring his consciousness in loving surrender to the consciousness of the Father, who was always present, seeking communion with his Son through his Spirit of love.

Jesus teaches us that prayer is fundamentally a loving listen-ing to God as he continually communicates his love to us at each moment. We pray when we are attentive to the presence of God, when we lift our hearts and minds to God's communicating presence. God does not begin and then cease to enter into this loving self-giving. His Son, Jesus, realized in his prayer that his Father surrounded him at every moment of his earthly existence with his Spirit. He opened himself to receive that "invasion" of his Father's goodness by yielding actively to whatever the Father was asking of him in each moment. Thus, Jesus prayed always in whatever he was engaged in doing.

Prayer, for Jesus, was not an activity in which he engaged before he did something else. It was a permanent, ever-increasing state of being turned inwardly toward the Father at every moment in loving trust and self-surrender. Prayer became synonymous with loving surrender based on childlike trust. "My son, attend to me, keep your eyes fixed on my advice" (Prv 23:26).

As Gold Is Purified by Fire

The First Epistle of St. Peter exhorts us to develop our God-given faith through trials, which can purify that faith as gold is purified by fire.

> God's power will guard you until the salvation which has been prepared is revealed at the end of time. This is a cause of great joy for you, even though you may for a short time have to bear being plagued by all sorts of trials; so that, when Jesus Christ is revealed, your faith will have been tested and proved like gold — only it is more precious than gold, which is corruptible even though it bears testing by fire — and then you will have praise and glory and honor (1 Pt 1:5–7).

Jesus was purified by trials, temptations and eventually death itself in order that he might reach the perfection of his trust in the loving goodness of his Father. The gospels present the peak of Jesus' holiness as an exodus or pass-over experience. He was tempted in his growth in holiness to hold on to his own life rather than to surrender his life on behalf of us sinners.

The temptations of Jesus undergone during the 40 days and nights he spent in the desert before he began his public life of preaching and healing, which would lead eventually to his death on the cross, are seen in the three synoptic gospels as symbols of how Jesus progressed in holiness by overcoming temptations to do his own will in opposition to that of his Father (see Mt 4:1–11; Mk 1:13; Lk 4:1–13).

The three temptations of Jesus in the desert are presented as trials that Jesus received from the Evil One to highlight Jesus' total attachment to his Father. Jesus is tempted to take the initiative away from the directing will of his Father in an aggressiveness that would deny God's sovereignty over him. He would refuse to yield to feed himself by anything but God's word. Power and glory over humble worship to God were rejected by Jesus' quotation from Deuteronomy 6:13: *"You must worship the Lord your God, and serve him alone"* (Lk 4:8). Finally, he claims his divine origin, not by presuming on God's power to protect him, but by an inner poverty of spirit that puts his whole dependence upon God's goodness. *"You must not put the Lord your God to the test"* (Lk 4:12).

Abandonment to the Father's Love

The story of Jesus' desert temptations is the story of his earthly life and struggle to allow his Father's love to enter into all his levels — conscious and unconscious. He progressively learned to let go of the control he could have exercised over his own human existence. He experienced at one and the same time the immense love of the Father for him in all details of his life. He also was moved by God's Spirit of love to return that love in an abandonment that would lead eventually to his ignominious death on the cross.

Especially in the agony in the Garden of Gethsemane and on the cross Jesus entered into the black darkness of his inner self, and there he struggled with the test of his personal identity in relationship with his heavenly Father. Was he to worship the Lord God and serve him alone? Or was he to yield to fear and doubt by grasping in self-centeredness to hold on to his life?

We see how trust developed in the garden trials of heaviness, fright, sorrow, disgust and loathing that came over him. Fear, a new experience for Jesus, came over him and he wished to run away from doing the manifested will of his Father. "Father,... if you are willing, take this cup away from me" (Lk 22:42). His sweat fell to the ground like great drops of blood. What a tremendous burst of love was generated in Jesus' soul as he trustingly surrendered himself to do only the Father's holy will: "Nevertheless, let your will be done, not mine!" (Lk 22:42).

The Dark Night

Trust admits of varying degrees of intensity as one surrenders himself or herself to seek whatever God's will at that moment may be revealing. *"Here I am! I am coming to obey your will"* (Heb 10:9).

But it is on the cross that Jesus learns the perfection of trust as he encounters the inner darkness that seeks like a swirling ocean surf to engulf him totally into meaninglessness through despair. Nowhere does the light of the Father's warm love for Jesus, his beloved Son, appear as he hangs in agony on the cross. There is only black darkness, chilling doubt.

Was he mistaken over all those years that his Father really loved Him? Was he really his only-begotten Son, of one same substance with the Father? Where is his Father, if he really loves him, especially now when he needs his comforting presence? Why does the Father treat him in this excruciating way? How did Jesus offend him?

Swirling black clouds of despair rise up. A cry of anguish: *"My God, my God, why have you deserted me?"* (Mk 15:34). Grasping for a shred of light, Jesus brings himself to a total surrender to the Father. He lets go of the last hold on his self-possession. He always sought to please his Father. Now Jesus returns his life to the Father with nothing in return of experienced love and his Father's goodness.

"Father, into your hands I commit my spirit" (Lk 23:46). Jesus passes over in his exodus into a blind abandonment into his Father's hands, who is now free to do with him whatever he wishes.

Jesus, obedient unto death, reaches a oneness with the Father through his childlike trust, which he never before experienced in his human consciousness. The Father glorifies him as his true Son, the perfect image of the Father's love for humanity.

Love Is Begotten by Trust

Jesus teaches us that trust is never a static resignation of himself to his Father's will. Love for another comes out of trust toward that person in a continued process of surrendering to that person in a desire to become more totally one. To love is to begin with a surrender to the good pleasure and happiness of the other.

To the degree that Jesus experiences his Father's active love for him in the details of his concrete human situation, to that degree, through trust in the Father's loving goodness, he strives in greater spontaneity and inner freedom to return his love to the Father.

Trust becomes an inventive process whereby Jesus is interiorly prompted to give in each moment more and more of his consciousness over to his Father. He seeks to surrender through a trust that will bring a ready obedience to do completely and perfectly all that Jesus perceives as a concrete expression of the Father's will in the form of commands. He seeks to trust even more as he strives to discover through the Spirit's enlightenment the wish of the Father in this present situation. But he goes beyond any human rationality to seek through his creative suffering to equal the self-emptying love of the Father toward him by inventing spontaneous expressions of his desire to give still more of himself in self-surrender.

Trust and Love Know No Bounds

In the continued experiences that Jesus had during his human existence on earth of his Father's infinite love for him, there grew up in his heart an ever-greater swelling of generosity and abandonment, like a cascading mountain stream gaining momentum and power as it approaches the sea. "As the Father has loved me, so I have loved you" (Jn 15:9).

The logic of the folly of the cross is no human logic. It cannot be understood by human minds, but only through the movement of the self-emptying Love of God, the Holy Spirit, leading Jesus to new heights of creative surrender to his Father. He wants eagerly to partake of this baptism of the Spirit of love, to be poured out as molten wax. Through complete trust in the Father, who can do whatever he wishes in Jesus' life, he desires to be dissolved of all self-containment in order to be united in complete oneness in love with his Father.

Perfect trust goes beyond the limitations of obedience to fulfill the expressed commands and wishes of the Father that are present to his consciousness. Jesus moves into this kind of trust, which grew throughout his lifetime: "For I always do what pleases him" (Jn 8:29). In his passion and in the excruciating, interior humiliations and utter abandonment by his Father, Jesus freely goes forth and desires to empty himself so as to equal in human form of suffering the self-emptying love of the Father toward him. "More darkness, more emptiness, more abandonment that I might the more trust in your perfect goodness and love toward me, your only Son!" could have been his cry as Jesus moved into the full expression of God's love in human form for all of us to look up and contemplate.

Jesus, Help Our Trust!

Such trust, in the face of trials that attack and seek to destroy whatever trust we bring before God, can only be realized as we, like Jesus, experience the outpoured love of the Father, even in such trials. This can come about only through the working of the Spirit of the risen Jesus. The Spirit alone will reveal the depths of the Father's love for each of us. He will give us the strength to trust in that love as, in the very context of trials and tribulations, we learn to act in a trust that corresponds to the love of the Father we have experienced through the Spirit.

We will begin to become Christians when, not only by the example of how Jesus learned to trust in trials, but by his powerful gift of the Spirit, we freely abandon ourselves totally to the Father in all things. In that Spirit, and through our active exercise of a trust similar to that of Jesus, we can live out the beautiful summary of how Jesus trusted the Father in all things.

> We know that by turning everything to their good God co-operates with all those who love him, with all those that he has called according to his purpose. They are the ones he chose specially long ago and intended to become true images of his Son, so that his Son might be the eldest of many brothers. He called those he intended for this; those he called he justified, and with those he justified he shared his glory (Rom 8:28–30).

CHAPTER 3

Be Not Afraid

Everyone the world over is continually discussing the important issue of peace. Yet how few of us human beings enjoy the peace Jesus promised to give his followers who would trust in him as God's true peace. "Peace I bequeath to you, my own peace I give you, a peace the world cannot give, this is my gift to you" (Jn 14:27).

We all eagerly desire true peace. Yet the plain truth in our hearts, in our families, neighborhoods, cities, countries, the world over is that there is no peace. With the prophet Jeremiah we can honestly say: "'Peace! Peace!' they say, but there is no peace" (Jer 6:14).

In the Old Testament the Hebrew word for peace, *shalom*, connotes the sense of being whole, intact, finished, complete. The noun means chiefly well-being, health, prosperity, wealth, numerous offspring, long life, victory over one's enemies and peaceful possession of the Promised Land. It refers not only to the individual's peace, but also to peace given to the collective people of God as a nation.

Jesus came not only to speak to us about peace but, as the Word of God, to create peace. He acts to bring about peace to individuals through his healing love, and through his disciples to extend such peaceful harmony throughout the world. "God is not a God of disorder but of peace" (1 Cor 14:33). "God has called us to peace" (1 Cor 7:15).

Yet, this peace, which he alone can give, cannot be had without a deep upheaval of all the carnal values that flow out of our sinful self-centeredness. To follow Jesus' way, which alone brings true peace, there is need of violence to whatever opposes our living in complete, loving submission to God and in loving our neighbor as we love ourselves. "Do not suppose that I have come to bring peace to the earth: it is not peace I have come to bring, but a sword" (Mt 10:34). Christ, the true prince of peace, is "a sign that is rejected" (Lk 2:34). His peace brings no comfort to us in our sinful tendency to cling to the illusory world we have created because we fear, more than anything else in our lives, to trust in a God we cannot see with our eyes and seemingly, but so foolishly, think we can control with our minds.

Fear Spawns More Fears

So often we seek in religion a false peace because we fear to give up our fears through absolute trust in an invisible God of love. God's awesome gift of himself to us through his Son Jesus in his Spirit comes to us in his gift of freedom. God pursues us in love but he also gives us the frightening power to say yes or no to his gift. We stand dizzily on the heights of the universe, tempted as Jesus was in the desert; we can bow in loving, trustful surrender to God's majesty and tender love as our eternal Father or walk away into the darkness of self-centered love.

In the legend of the Grand Inquisitor, Feodor Dostoevsky has the 16th-century Inquisitor address the imprisoned Jesus, who had come back to this earth to call men and women again to true freedom:

> Instead of taking men's freedom from them, Thou didst make it greater than ever! Didst Thou forget that man prefers peace, and even death, to freedom of choice in the knowledge of good and evil?...In place of the rigid ancient law, man must hereafter with free heart decide for himself what is good and what is evil, having only Thy image before him as his guide. But didst Thou not know that he would at last reject even Thy image and Thy trust, if he is weighed down with the fearful burden of free choice? *(The Brothers Karamazov).*

The majority of Christians want a religion of "miracles, mystery and authority." Freedom demands too great a responsibility to choose according to the image of Jesus and his truth. Too often Christians prefer to hug their fears and scream if anyone, even God, were to take them away!

I believe that the greatest psychic enslavement is fear. It is the opposite of faith, hope and love, given us only by God's Holy Spirit. The message of Christianity is that given by John in his first epistle: "In love there can be no fear, but fear is driven out by perfect love: because to fear is to expect punishment, and anyone who is afraid is still imperfect in love" (1 Jn 4:18).

When we fail to trust in God's love manifested in Jesus Christ and made known to us through faith by the Holy Spirit, the fears with which we were born only spawn greater fears. Fear can be about innumerable objects. It is the state of fear from which we must be delivered by Jesus Christ, for often the objects that we fear are only in our minds. To find healing we must discover the root of our fear, which is so often centered in a lack of faith and trust in God's loving care for us.

Fear Not

How often Jesus spoke words of confidence and loving strength to those burdened with fear. To the frightened disciples locked up in the Upper Room after his death, he uttered these fear-dissolving words: "Peace be with you! ...Why are you so agitated, and why are these doubts rising in your hearts?" (Lk 24:37–38). On the stormy lake, Jesus asked the same disciples: "Why are you so frightened, you men of little faith?" (Mt 8:26). He told all who were laboring under the heavy weight of any fear and were overburdened that he would give them rest (Mt 11:29).

Above all, he came to reveal to us that we have a loving Father, who numbers every hair on our heads. We are not to worry excessively in the light of this great revelation, for if God takes care of the birds of the air and clothes the lilies of the fields, how much more, Jesus insists, will our Father in heaven take care of all our future needs? The conclusion is, therefore: "There is no need to be afraid, little flock, for it has pleased your Father to give you the kingdom" (Lk 12:32).

Crippling Fears

How often we say in prayer: "Yes, Lord, I truly trust in your providential care over me. You are omnipotent, omniscient and omnipresent. You are love itself, and you always act out of your own goodness." Yet, we find ourselves over and over lacking in trust, as our many fears, especially of the unknown ahead of us, destroy our childlike trust in God's active goodness and love for us.

This cripples us, preventing us from living dynamic, decisive lives; we are stalemated into a no-decision attitude. We procrastinate, fearing to make decisions rooted in deep faith and trust of the hidden God who truly loves us. We pray and intellectually give our assent to what the psalmist says:

> Trust in Yahweh and do what is good,
> make your home in the land and live in peace;
> make Yahweh your only joy
> and he will give you what your heart desires.
> Commit your fate to Yahweh,
> trust in him and he will act:
> making your virtue clear as the light,
> your integrity as bright as noon (Ps 37:3–6).

Yet we find ourselves returning to our old fears and inventing new ones. Where do these fears, which obstruct our complete trust in God's providence, come from?

> For example, our mothers stamp fear upon us before we are born, and continue to do it after we are born, and until we have grown old enough to fear for ourselves. They create disease for us through their fears of diseases until we get old enough to create our own diseases. And that wretched fear follows us from the cradle to the grave. We are afraid we shall not succeed in business, and we create our own failures. We are afraid we shall not have the money to pay our bills for the current month, and we generally lack something because we have created that lack. We fear bad luck, disaster and death, and it is a wonder that man has not swept himself off the face of the earth through his fearful creations. The offspring of fear are the creatures and creations of this objective mind, and the subjective mind, which is within objective mind, accepts the unfortunate creations, believes the misrepresentations, and unites its own forces with those of the objective mind in bringing the pictured calamities into real, external existence (S. Triton, *The Magic of Space*).

Not only do we wallow in our own personal fears, but cosmic fears rise up and haunt us with nightmarish possibilities of nuclear explosions capable of destroying all life on this planet. We live in fear of the Soviets and the Chinese. And they, in turn, fear us. Earthquakes, tornadoes, droughts, epidemics are very real to us through rapid news coverage, filling us with unconscious fears that such cataclysms will soon befall us. Fear breeds fear. All too often our fears are fears of fear itself.

Knowing Our Fears

Like haunting specters that swirl madly within our unconscious, these fears mount to the degree that we do not get in touch with them and then bravely eliminate them by firm, rational action, rooted in God's revealed love, his truth, in which we place all our trust.

We become liberated from the bondage of fear when we can look at the fear itself in terms not only of our own strength, but also the strength of God. If the fear has come from our own conscious or unconscious mind, it will be dissolved by pouring into those psychic areas the healing power of God's vision of reality to dispel the projections of the insecure false ego.

But the great question is: Are we ready and willing to let go of these fears that allow us an illusory and enslaving comfort and security? To let go of such fears is a true dying process that many of us are not quite ready to undergo. Many of us prefer living in the cave of fearful shadows brought about by self-centered projections instead of surrendering in childlike faith to Jesus' revelation that "the Father himself loves you for loving me and believing that I came from God" (Jn 16:27).

Who can adequately describe the enslavement of worries born out of fear, anxiety, dread or regret? How crippling is the anger that bursts out in violent verbal or even physical attacks against others, or is allowed to eat away our inner integration through repression? Anger with its levels of rage, fury, irritation, revenge, jealousy, envy and scorn is one of the most enslaving signs of the false ego to seek power and domination over others.

Fear of what others may think holds us in its captivity, draining us of our ability to communicate in freedom and love with others. We react through an inferiority complex, a sick, wishy-washy yielding to stronger personalities or the inevitability of circumstances. We destroy the reputation of others by sharp criticism, gossip, calumnies and slanders.

An inordinate desire for approval and praise from others fills us with vanity and crippling pride. We resort to lies, cheating, playing roles, all to create an impression that deep down we know is untrue.

Hatred is a strong emotion rooted in fear, for we hate what we fear. We hate those who threaten us. Hate destroys human communication and growth into true humanity by love. All hatred destroys communion in love. It isolates us from one another. Hatred can only be dissolved by forgiving love, based on trust of God's mercy that is above all his works. Jesus taught us that we are to forgive and to love even our enemies, those who hate us and seek to do evil to us (Lk 6:27–35).

God's Divine Providence

We can be healed only by true faith in God's active, guiding providence in our lives, even in the midst of our fears, brokenness and sins. Jesus is the Way that leads us to the Truth that our heavenly Father truly loves us as imaged by the love Jesus has shown for us. It is acting on this truth of God's infinite, perfect, active love for us in every moment of our human existence that will bring us into peace, true healing and integration (Jn 14:6).

Our Father is not content to be a passive witness in our lives. He is an active doer out of his natural goodness as God. By his uncreated energies of love through his Son and his Holy Spirit, the Father intervenes intensely and mysteriously in every detail of our lives.

Being all-powerful, the Father does take the initiative and can act independently of us. Yet he respects our free will and seeks to "allure" us by his goodness to make decisions out of our inner dignity of being his children. His providence continually watches over us and exercises a beneficent influence at all times upon us.

True children of God realize in life's circumstances that they have no strength of their own. In all moments we are to confess our weakness to do good by ourselves. We know with St. Paul that all our strength is in God through Christ Jesus. True strength begins with a realized conviction that we ourselves are weak, but our very weakness confessed becomes our strength because we lovingly surrender to God in all things.

So I shall be very happy to make my weaknesses my special boast so that the power of Christ may stay over me, and that is why I am quite content with my weaknesses, and with insults, hardships, persecutions, and the agonies I go through for Christ's sake. For it is when I am weak that I am strong (2 Cor 12:9–10).

The fruit that our Father wishes us to bring forth is a constant, loving, trustful submission and obedience to his commands and desires. To believe that the Father truly loves us, as Jesus reveals, and that he does all things out of love is the basis for our childlike trust and complete surrender to his guiding providence.

> I need only say, "I am slipping,"
> and your love, Yahweh, immediately supports me;
> and in the middle of all my troubles
> you console me and make me happy (Ps 94:18–19).

> Your decrees will never alter;
> holiness will distinguish your house,
> Yahweh, forever and ever (Ps 93:5).

God is truly our only rock of strength. Faultless are his deeds.

> He is the Rock, his work is perfect,
>   for all his ways are Equity.
> A God faithful, without unfairness,
>   Uprightness itself and Justice (Dt 32:4).

> Yahweh is righteous,
>   my rock in whom no fault is to be found! (Ps 92:15).

God Causes All Things to Exist

The revelation found in the Old and New Testaments attests to the foundational truth upon which we can build our trust in God's loving providence. That truth is simply that the will of God is the cause of all that exists. God cannot cause evil but only good, since he is goodness and love by his very nature. He creates all things and sees that they are very good. He has care over all his creatures. "For there is no god, other than you, who cares for every thing, to whom you might have to prove that you never judged unjustly" (Wis 12:13–14).

No human person can have the knowledge to understand the mysteries of God's providential guidance of all things, nor can any creature stand up and question why God acts. With Job, we can only surrender to God's wisdom in guiding all things well. With Job we too can answer:

> I know that you are all-powerful:
>   what you conceive, you can perform.
> I am the man who obscured your designs
>   with my empty-headed words.
> I have been holding forth on matters I cannot
>   understand,
>   on marvels beyond me and my knowledge....
> I knew you then only by hearsay;
>   but now, having seen you with my own eyes,
> I retract all I have said,
>   and in dust and ashes I repent (Jb 42:2–6).

God Acts in Wisdom

We can never understand the ways of the Lord, nor comprehend why he acts in any given manner, especially when he lovingly seeks to punish us and discipline us so that we can repent from our arrogant blindness and the desire to follow our own will. Our sole answer must be to surrender to God in childlike trust in his goodness to act always for our happiness.

How beautifully Isaiah the prophet describes this loving trust we must have in God:

> For you hid your face from us
> and gave us up to the power of our sins.
> And yet, Yahweh, you are our Father;
> we the clay, you the potter,
> we are all the work of your hands (Is 64:7–8).

Truly, we believe that God does all things in wisdom. "Yahweh, what variety you have created, arranging everything so wisely! Earth is completely full of things you have made" (Ps 104:24). St. Basil of the fourth century gives expression to the common teaching of the early Fathers when he writes: "We ought then to ponder well on this thought, that we are the work of a good Workman, and that He dispenses and distributes to us all good things, great and small, with the wisest providence, so that there is nothing bad, nothing that could even be conceived better."

God Is Good Even When He Disciplines Us

We will develop this important topic in another chapter. But in dealing with our fears, which hold us back from total, childlike trust in God, it is important that we consider everything as a part of God's wisdom and reason if we are to drive out fears by abandonment to God's goodness and omnipotence.

Jesus clearly lived such trust toward his heavenly Father in accepting the sufferings of his passion and death. And he clearly taught us to accept God as loving, even when he, the Vinedresser, prunes us. By such a purification, which may bring us much suffering, the heavenly Father seeks only that we may receive more abundantly his divine life.

> Every branch in me that bears no fruit
> he cuts away,
> and every branch that does bear fruit he prunes
> to make it bear even more....
> It is to the glory of my Father that you should bear much
> fruit,
> and then you will be my disciples (Jn 15:1-2, 8).

Our belief that all things, especially sufferings and trials and persecutions, truly can work unto good for those who love the Lord will dissolve all fears and allow us to accept such crosses out of a deep trust in God's goodness and wisdom operating in all things. We will learn to trust in God who, as St. Paul teaches, is always faithful and will never permit us to be tempted or afflicted beyond our strength (1 Cor 10:13).

We will continue in faith that "we all have to experience many hardships...before we enter the kingdom of God" (Acts 14:22). Our Christian faith and the trust that should be ours in accepting the Father's purification of ourselves in order to become more fully divinized participators of his very own nature is clearly outlined in Hebrews:

Suffering is part of your *training*; God is treating you as his *sons*. Has there ever been any *son* whose father did not *train* him? ...Our human fathers were thinking of this short life when they punished us, and could only do what they thought best; but he does it all for our own good, so that we may share his own holiness. Of course, any punishment is most painful at the time, and far from pleasant; but later, in those on whom it has been used, it bears fruit in peace and goodness (Heb 12:7–11).

Healing of Our Fears

Before we can truly trust in God's goodness and love, always operating in each moment of our lives, especially in painful sufferings, we need not only to be aware of our many and deep-rooted fears, but also to be healed of them. Freed from the obstacles that prevent God's love from filling us with trust, we can live in the constant childlike trust as a state of being toward our loving Father.

The gospels present past historical moments in the earthly life of Jesus when he healed the sick and the maimed, drove away the fears from the hearts of the fearful and the suffering, and reconciled the sinners to his Father's love. Yet, since the gospels are teachings of how to live a Christian life based on the beliefs of the first disciples of Jesus, he still continues in his risen presence to do to us, his modern followers, what he did to all who came to him in the hope of being totally healed and brought into a new creation in his life.

As we tremble in fears that whip us into isolation away from God's real world of providential, caring love, there is hope for us because of Jesus, the Divine Physician, who can free us from our fears.

But faith means being grasped by a power that is greater than we are, a power that shakes us and turns us, and transforms us and heals us. Surrender to this power is faith. The people whom Jesus could heal and can heal are those who did and do this self-surrender to the healing power in Him. They surrendered their persons, split, contradicting themselves, disgusted and despairing about themselves, hateful of themselves and, therefore, hostile towards everybody else; afraid of life, burdened with guilt feeling, accusing and excusing themselves, fleeing from others into loneliness, fleeing from themselves to others, trying finally to escape from the threats of existence into the painful and deceptive safety of mental and bodily disease. As such beings, they surrendered to Jesus and this surrender is what we call faith.... We belong to these people, if we are grasped by the new reality which has appeared in Him. We have His healing power ourselves (Paul Tillich, The New Being, pp. 38–39).

Jesus, the Divine Physician

On every page of the gospels we see how Jesus stretched out his hands of healing, and the sick felt the love of God pour into their broken bodies, minds and hearts. He was the Son of God and they, for a brief moment, hung suspended between the darkness of their own isolation and the light of the freeing truth that they were sons and daughters of God himself. As they yielded to the presence of Jesus' love in their lives, they felt wholeness come over them. Their fears were swept away as the tide sweeps out into the depths of the ocean the debris that clutters up the coastal sands.

That same living Jesus wishes to pour out his Spirit of love into our hearts; we need only consent to receive this love. He wishes to heal us in the deepest layers of our being, our spirit, from all our haunting and crippling fears by giving us faith to let go of these fears and guilt and all the unnatural reactions that follow and to begin to live in his new life.

Through his Holy Spirit he opens our spiritual eyes to his new vision. In this vision we can know through faith, hope and love that we are really God's children.

Think of the love that the Father has lavished on us,
by letting us be called God's children;
and that is what we are....
My dear people, we are already the children of God
but what we are to be in the future has not yet been revealed (1 Jn 3:1–2).

Healing and the Prayer of the Heart

To enter into our inner being, to come to the center wherein the Trinity dwells as the ground of our being, we must embrace a psychic silence. It is more than a mere refraining from speaking words to God. It is an inward movement into what scripture calls the heart of a person. It is going beyond the controlled knowledge we entertain of ourselves and even of God and the world around us.

We have all heard and perhaps have adapted certain methods of entering into "still-pointedness" at the core of our being. Transcendental Meditation (TM) uses Hindu meditation techniques. Zen Buddhism, Silva Mind-Control and a host of mind-expanding systems, along with hypnosis, use similar methods of entering into a relaxed, more total awareness of the deeper layers of the conscious and unconscious mind.

For Eastern Christians, who inherited a centering process that employs the Christian mantra of the *Jesus Prayer*, the heart is opened to the healing power of the indwelling Trinity. Such a Christian form of healing prayer must always be guided by God's revelation in scripture and the teachings of the church to avoid the release of even greater fears and anxieties and to bring us more directly into the healing power of Jesus the Healer.

Trust is developed even as we encounter such repressed fears and hurts from the past, but always in the loving and healing power of Jesus. As we yield to the indwelling Trinity and allow ourselves to be loved as children of God, loved infinitely by God himself in Christ Jesus, we experience a movement into new freedom as children of God, loved infinitely by God himself in Christ Jesus through his Spirit. Our potential for *being* expands into a realized consciousness, measured by more trusting abandonment in complete surrender to God's holy will.

We can truly experience being healed of our fears and anxieties. How exciting to feel the healing power of God's love dissolve the tight bonds of slavery from so much of the past, from so much that we never even recognized as a source of non-life in us.

Healing Prayer

In order to pray in our hearts and beyond our own perceptual knowledge, we need to come into the first stage of relaxation, namely, to place ourselves in a position of physical quiet and harmony. To bring to the Lord our deep fears to be healed and replaced by childlike trust in God's perfect love and mercy, our body with all of its nerves, muscles and organs must be brought into a relaxed wholeness. For this we should choose a very relaxed position, either sitting or standing. Most people relax best when sitting down. Some might prefer the relaxed but disciplined yoga position of the lotus or semi-lotus. Most, however, can attain bodily relaxation by sitting on a straight chair in such a way that the spinal cord is straight up and down with no hunching of the shoulders.

Proper breathing is important in attaining and holding an inner state of relaxation. Breathing diaphragmatically puts us into an inner rhythm that allows the body to move into submission to the higher soul-powers. To breathe in this fashion, one inhales and becomes aware of the diaphragm muscle in the abdominal cavity extending outwardly. As one exhales the diaphragm moves toward the spine. Back and forth in such oppositional breathing, one feels oneself sinking into a state of great physical and psychic relaxation. One is able to let faith exercise itself on a larger level of receptivity to God's movement. One is now *listening* to God and giving him the freedom to speak his Word when and how he wishes.

Clearing the Mind

So many fears and worries are lodged in our minds! When we come to pray, our freedom to surrender completely to God's "take-over" is inhibited. Thus we need to bring our minds to a still-pointedness or a oneness with the mind of Jesus Christ. Here we all have to experiment and develop our own methods of clearing the mind.

I like to suggest a descending movement where the meditator imagines taking an elevator from the 20th floor of a building down slowly to the basement. As the elevator passes each floor,

the meditator becomes more relaxed by letting go of all bodily
and psychic tensions in order to arrive in deep faith before the
risen Lord.

Our Spirit and God's Spirit Pray Together

In the presence of the risen Jesus the meditator fixates on a
mantra that is mentally recited over and over and synchronized
with breathing. Such a breath-prayer might be: "Jesus, mercy."
One breathes in the name of *Jesus* and exhales the word *mercy.*
Another suggested breath-prayer in keeping with the theme of
this book would be "Jesus — I trust in you." Thus the meditator
keeps focused on the presence of Jesus, or on the Trinity —
Father, Son and Holy Spirit.

This is praying in the Spirit, as St. Paul teaches us:

> The Spirit too comes to help us in our weakness. For
> when we cannot choose words in order to pray properly,
> the Spirit himself expresses our plea in a way that could
> never be put into words, and God who knows everything
> in our hearts knows perfectly well what he means, and
> that the pleas of the saints expressed by the Spirit are
> according to the mind of God (Rom 8:26–27).

It is when the meditator feels completely one with the loving
power of God, personalized and turned toward him or her, that
the meditator begins to receive complete healing from God. Let
me now summarize the steps to such healing of our fears unto
greater trust in God.

1. Select a quiet place, free from noise and interruptions. The
    best time is usually in early morning before the activities of
    the day or before meals, but not after them, or when one is
    very fatigued.

2. Take a position that is comfortable, yet disciplined enough to
    prevent sleep or undue distractions. This can be sitting on a
    cushion on the floor or on a straight-back chair.

3. Localize yourself in the presence of the Trinity by making acts
    of faith, adoration, hope and love.

4. Begin to breathe consciously. Feel the breath entering your lungs and follow slowly its exhalation. Synchronize your inhalation and exhalation with the opposite movement of your diaphragm. Lengthen your breathing into calm, long breaths. Feel yourself relaxing.

5. Consciously start from the head and go through all parts of the body, commanding each part to give up any tension and replace it with complete relaxation. Enjoy the feeling of becoming whole physically.

6. Descend by any technique that is meaningful and yields good results into your "heart," the deeper layers of your consciousness where, beyond words and images, you will meet God dwelling within you as the Trinity — Father, Son and Holy Spirit. (I have suggested above the technique of going down the "elevator.")

7. The most important part of this healing exercise consists in the deep faith that Jesus Christ is present and still healing all who truly believe in his healing love. "Do not be afraid; it is I" (Rv 1:17). It is imperative in the healing of our fears and anxieties to approach the Divine Physician with that faith that he himself insisted upon:

> Have faith in God. I tell you solemnly, if anyone says to this mountain, "Get up and throw yourself into the sea," with no hesitation in his heart but believing that what he says will happen, it will be done for him. I tell you, therefore: everything you ask and pray for, believe that you have it already, and it will be yours. And when you stand in prayer, forgive whatever you have against anybody, so that your Father in heaven may forgive your failings too (Mk 11:22–25).

8. The first element in such healing through childlike faith and trust consists in forgiving others any injury they may have caused you. Let go of any animosity toward any other. Feel a oneness as the love of God's Spirit unites you with that person or persons.

9. Finally, picture Jesus touching that area of the body, soul or
    spirit that needs healing. This might be a relationship with
    someone absent. See yourself already healed and living in a
    new-founded trusting love toward all others. Begin to thank
    God for such a healing. Know it is already being done as
    you believe. What is most important is that we surrender
    all our fears, known and unknown, to the healing power of
    Jesus Christ.

Leaving such prayer, we should entertain a spirit of great
gratitude, knowing that God has truly answered our prayer. We
are healed! And for this we thank God all that day. We act on the
conviction that God has heard the prayer and is progressively
healing us by giving us deeper trust, which is dissolving our fears
and self-centeredness.

Our ability to rejoice and give praise to God in all prosperity
and in all sufferings depends on our childlike trust in God's great
love for us in Christ Jesus. Adversities purify our loving praise and
self-surrender so that we praise God always solely because he is
good and holy. He is simply love! Adversities allow us to humble
ourselves before God that he may raise us up to a new union of
faith, hope and love with him. We will then live daily the
exhortation of St. Peter:

Bow down, then, before the power of God now, and he
will raise you up on the appointed day; *unload* all *your
worries on to him*, since he is looking after you (1 Pt 5:6–7).

CHAPTER 4

Trust in God's Forgiving Love

One temptation that will haunt us from time to time, and especially on our deathbed, is whether all the sins we have committed in our lifetime have really been forgiven by God. "How can we really be sure?" is a question all of us, perhaps, have asked ourselves. We wonder: Did I confess my sins properly? Didn't I withhold certain sins in confession out of shame? Perhaps I rationalized my way out of certain sins, justifying myself only to be tormented as I grew older by the thought of a possible hell for all eternity as my just due.

Martin Luther, the initiator of the Protestant Reformation in Germany and founder of Lutheranism, was tormented by such scrupulous questionings. He wrote that as an Augustinian monk he was torn by doubts about his own justification and whether he eventually would be saved. He records his "tower experience," when he locked himself up in the tower in the Wittenburg monastery and refused to come down until he received from God the certainty that he was saved by faith in the blood of Jesus and that his sins were truly forgiven.

Perhaps most Christians are in the greatest need of trust in God's forgiveness of their personal sins. We must, for true integration and health of body, soul and spirit, begin always by accepting our past sins and guilt and humbly bring them to God's merciful forgiveness in order to receive from him inner peace and healing.

But our sins can be treated by us in various ways. Some Christians entertain lax consciences and an ability easily to rationalize themselves out of any guilt or need for reform. Such people presume too much on God's mercy. They have read scripture and heard sermons about God's mercy. But they conveniently forget the necessity of a conversion by turning away from living selfishly toward God and neighbor.

Fear and Scrupulosity

Other Christians, through faulty religious upbringing and basic character fashioned in family and school training, develop a scrupulous conscience. Among many sincere and sensitive religious persons scrupulosity, although not from God, can be a severe temptation lasting for long periods of time.

Scrupulosity can never be from God, for it cloaks a subtle temptation to pride and a complete lack of trust in God's mercy. It is one of the worst trials that one can undergo in the spiritual life; it renders true prayer inefficacious due to a self-absorption that cannot be pleasing to God.

Scrupulosity does not spring from a delicacy of conscience and a desire to please God, but rather from ignorance, error or defective judgment. Usually such people refuse to obey both their spiritual director and the common teaching of the church in such a matter.

For such people, there usually is no distinction between imperfections and serious sins. The terrifying judgment of God is accentuated with little trust in his infinite love and mercy. Slight faults can be magnified to gigantic crimes. The conscience becomes raw and tender, like bare feet that walk for miles over stony roads.

Such people cannot be their own judges; they must submit to the prudent judgment of a confessor-director. Such a person usually has inherited a melancholic disposition or is extremely suspicious by nature. Scrupulosity, therefore, is a subtle form of self-love or spiritual self-absorption. Still, such a state can be used by God to bring such persons into a deeper abandonment and trust.

Accepting Our Sinfulness and Guilt

Dr. Karl Menninger once thought that sin with its accompanying guilt was a mere myth from an unenlightened age. He changed his mind after years of directing his famous clinic for mental health. In *Whatever Became of Sin?* he points out that all of our human acts partake of some voluntary, as well as involuntary, choosing. True mental health, he insists, demands that we achieve as much responsibility as possible in our acts.

In all of the laments and reproaches made by our seers and prophets, one misses any mention of "sin," a word which used to be a veritable watchword of prophets. It was a word once in everyone's mind, but now rarely, if ever, heard. Does that mean that no sin is involved in all our troubles — sin with an "I" in the middle? Is no one any longer guilty of anything? Guilty perhaps of a sin that could be repented and repaired or atoned for? Is it only that someone may be stupid or sick or criminal — or asleep? Wrong things are being done, we know; tares are being sown in the wheat field at night. But is no one responsible, no one answerable for these acts? Anxiety and depression we all acknowledge, and even vague guilt feelings; but has no one committed any sins? (p. 13).

Scriptural Sense of Sin

Christians in the West have formulated sin as a deliberate act done against God's laws with full consent. Today psychologists and psychiatrists, through depth psychology, are making us aware of the many hidden forces that lie as so much smoldering lava deep within our unconscious.

Today theologians are relating the powerful teaching of original sin to the forces inherited in the genetic programming found in our collective unconscious. In John's gospel this collective solidarity in sinfulness is called the sin of the world. This is the brokenness of the whole world that groans in travail and goes far beyond the mere totaling of all our individual sins. It refers to the sin of humanity as a united community in sinfulness.

Sin in the Old and New Testaments usually refers to any obstacle of brokenness within us that prevents us from hitting the mark. The Hebrew words, *het'* and *hatta't*, which are translated in the New Testament by the Greek word, *hamartia*, mean literally "to miss the mark." Sin thus embraces anything deliberate or indeliberate, regardless of how it came into our life-experiences, that prevents a human being, or the collective people of God, from living with God as the Center. It is failure to attain one's goal or end. Thus sin is denying God's truth, that he truly loves us and meets us in his merciful, forgiving love in all the details of our human existence. It is unreality insofar as it is considered "non-action" in regard to the "real" action that brings eternal fulfillment to the individual person or community.

In the New Testament sin can refer to a single act, or a state or condition, or a cosmic power. But what is so important in our fighting sin and its accompanying guilt and all its fears is trusting in God's forgiving love. This is the fundamental, Christian belief, the cornerstone of the Good News, that God has sent his own Son to conquer and destroy sin in the lives of those who believe in him as the Son of God and the Savior for us, the One who heals us of the ravages of sin.

Have Mercy on Me, a Sinner

The first step in a true conversion toward integration and coming into a deeper union with God and neighbor in love comes when we have the honesty and courage to confront our broken-ness and accept our responsibility for that something which is false, unreal, unauthentic in the way we approach God, in the way we habitually look at ourselves and at others. It is a question we need to ask ourselves, not once, but continually throughout our whole lifetime. "Will I stay inside myself, groping for ways in which I can allow God to be truly 'my God' instead of running 'outside' to be diverted from the call of God to new life?"

Gabriel Marcel, the great French philosopher, writes about the need we have of distractions to keep us away from the horrendous task of getting in touch with our sinfulness, guilt and fears:

> When we are at rest, we find ourselves almost inevitably put in the presence of our own inner emptiness, and this very emptiness is in reality intolerable to us. But there is more, there is the fact that through this emptiness we inevitably become aware of the misery of our condition, as "a condition so miserable," says Pascal, "that nothing can console us when we think about it carefully." Hence, the necessity of diversion (*Problematic Man*, p. 100).

What fears rise up like specters out of the mist and fog of our past! What raw experiences trigger anger, hatred, unforgiveness! What moods of depression, melancholy and loneliness come over us when we reflect on the wasted parts of our life! We see what sinful tendencies lie deep within us, what heinous evil acts we are capable of committing. We see the stranglehold of past habits exercising their enslavement over us. God lets a soft light of what-could-have-been shine into our broken darkness as we see the many areas of omissions, of good deeds not done, of God's gentle whispers unheeded.

With St. Paul we can cry out to God:

In my inmost self I dearly love God's Law, but I can see that my body follows a different law that battles against the law which my reason dictates. This is what makes me a prisoner of that law of sin which lives inside my body.

What a wretched man I am! Who will rescue me from this body doomed to death? Thanks be to God through Jesus Christ our Lord! (Rom 7:22–25).

Once we have the courage to have a healthy disgust with our eating of "the husks the pigs were eating" (Lk 15:16), we become more open to respond in urgent faith to believe in Jesus Christ as the Savior, who alone can take away our sins. We earnestly begin to trust in God's invitation to come back home and accept his forgiving love.

Come back to me with all your heart,
fasting, weeping, mourning.
Let your hearts be broken, not your garments torn,
turn to Yahweh your God again,
for he is all tenderness and compassion,
slow to anger, rich in graciousness,
and ready to relent (Jl 2:12–13).

In my priestly ministry the saddest experience for me is to witness the tremendous doubt and lack of trust in God's forgiving love as brought to us by Jesus Christ and his Holy Spirit. If we believe that God is love and mercifully cares for all our needs, why do we doubt that he will really forgive all our sins?

We need more than an intellectual assent to the truth that God's forgiving mercy came down and dwelt among us in his Son, Jesus Christ. We need to respond with all our heart to his call to repent and believe in him, the Way, the Truth and the Life, who alone can bring us healing and salvation. As he preached to the multitudes in Palestine, so he announces the Good News in our lives that precedes a true conversion. "The time has come," he said, "and the kingdom of God is close at hand. Repent, and believe the Good News" (Mk 1:15).

The anxiety, fear and disgust, as we confront our existence in the light of our "non-being," is more than a mere reflection on death and a cry for immortal life. It is an ontological nostalgia to leave the "husks the pigs were eating" and return home to our heavenly Father and thus discover our true selves in our loving obedience to him. It is the soft dew of God's grace falling upon the hard desert floor of our hearts to stir the seeds planted there when God created us "in the image of himself" (Gn 1:27).

There is hope for us that we do not have to continue living on such a low level of existence, riddled by fears and guilt, separated from all the persons whom we daily meet in a suspicion of threatening attack that makes us defensive and forces us to hide behind masks and walls that fill us with greater fears.

Proclaiming the Kingdom

Jesus invites us to repent of living in illusory desires as do those who have not heard the Good News. He releases his Spirit of love within us so we may desire to have a part with him and to share, even now in our earthly exile, his eternal life by living no longer separated from God as our Center, and united with our neighbor and the world around us in his loving Spirit.

The Good News that Jesus preached and still holds out to all who would freely accept his call to repentance is that God is the loving Father of all human beings. He is filled with infinite mercy and forgiving love. He does not look to the sins or falsity in our lives, but he brings his healing love to all who are lonely and desolate. He gives hope to the hopeless. His perfect love, experienced in the hearts of those who turn back in repentance to the Lord, casts out all fear (1 Jn 4:18).

> And you were dead, through the crimes and the sins in which you used to live when you were following the way of this world, obeying the ruler who governs the air, the spirit who is at work in the rebellious. We all were among

them too in the past, living sensual lives, ruled entirely by our own physical desires and our own ideas; so that by nature we were as much under God's anger as the rest of the world. But God loved us with so much love that he was generous with his mercy: when we were dead through our sins, he brought us to life with Christ — it is through grace that you have been saved — and raised us up with him and gave us a place with him in heaven, in Christ Jesus.

This was to show for all ages to come, through his goodness towards us in Christ Jesus, how infinitely rich he is in grace. Because it is by grace that you have been saved, through faith; not by anything of your own, but by a gift from God; not by anything that you have done, so that nobody can claim the credit. We are God's work of art, created in Christ Jesus to live the good life as from the beginning he had meant us to live it (Eph 2:1–10).

We Cannot Save Ourselves

How difficult it is for us Westerners, who are like the busy Martha, always anxious about what we must do to be saved. We feel uncomfortable in the role of Mary, as she sat at the feet of the Lord. We seem to be driven to prove we are worthwhile by what we do, by our accomplishments. Yet we forget that our "nature" can never stand independently of God's permeating graces at all times. Every gift, every talent and ability to do comes from God. "It is in him that we live, and move, and exist" (Acts 17:28). St. James exhorts us to recognize God as the source of all good: "It is all that is good, everything that is perfect, which is given us from above; it comes down from the Father of all light" (Jas 1:17).

We cannot do things thinking we can barter ourselves into salvation. We will enter into the healing process called salvation only when we realize we cannot heal ourselves or merit by our works the gift of God's love. Only when a recuperating alcoholic recognizes that he or she has a problem and cannot bring about his or her own healing does a new life begin to open up. Such a new life becomes realized only when there is faith in the healing power of an infinite force of love, God himself, who accepts a person's brokenness and replaces the need for alcohol by new self-esteem in the light of a loving community.

So it is with us all. Only when we crack through our false ego, which insists everything is all right and the others around us are the neurotic ones, can we begin to receive the new and eternal life of God. We, only in God's love and power of the Spirit, can stop living the lie and the illusions that keep us separated from a vengeful God and from our neighbor.

God's Unconditional Love

Then we will begin to open ourselves in earnest to receive God's unconditional love, which is always available and active from God's side. He does not have to come to us. It is we who come to his loving and healing presence. It is we who have to allow his mercy and grace to dissipate the darkness of our fearful self and replace it with our true self in the conscious living, no longer we ourselves, but letting Christ live in us, as St. Paul discovered in his conversion.

When our foolish and false pride is shaken and we enter into a true poverty of spirit or authentic humility, we put ourselves continually into the world of God's forgiving mercy and constant love that knows no end. Then Jesus Christ becomes our sole strength. Our very weaknesses become no longer obstacles, but the point where God meets us in his omnipotence, omniscience and omnipresence. St. Paul summarized this essential characteristic at the heart of every true and ongoing conversion before the strength of God's forgiving love:

> So I shall be very happy to make my weaknesses my special boast so that the power of Christ may stay over me, and that is why I am quite content with my weaknesses, and with persecutions, and the agonies I go through for Christ's sake. For it is when I am weak that I am strong (2 Cor 12:9–10).

A Trusting Hope

It is especially in our hope in God's forgiving us all our sins and making us justified or divinized children of God through his Spirit that we see the greatest reason for trusting in God's mercy toward us in our sinfulness. The basic reason for the absolute and certain trust we can have that God loves us lies in the hope the Holy Spirit of the risen Jesus infuses into our hearts.

Hope is the confidence that we have that God will give us all the help necessary to attain our eternal destiny. He will take care of all our needs and will never abandon us for a moment. Because of this hope, we can confidently surrender our lives and our future and that of the entire universe to God, who will forgive us our sins and turn all misfortunes and evils to our eternal happiness. St. Paul describes this hope from the Holy Spirit: "May the God of hope bring you such joy and peace in your faith that the power of the Holy Spirit will remove all bounds to hope" (Rom 15:13).

Our Christian faith gives to the world a concept of hope for all humans and for the total universe that is rooted in God's fidelity. In the *Hesed* Covenant, which God established first with Abraham and then through Moses with God's chosen people in the desert, God promised to become involved with his people. He condescends with his active mercy, which is never a concept of a God with utter detachment "forgiving" the errors of his people.

God is *grace*, a free, self-giving, serving action that flows out of God's very own nature. God truly seeks to give himself to his people at every moment of their existence. He will protect them and restore to them full prosperity, granting them happiness as the fulfillment of all their desires.

The chosen people, the *anawim* or *remnant* of those faithful to God, responded with trustful confidence because they hoped in God. They trusted in his revealed Word and acted on it. St. Paul points out that Abel, Enoch, Noah, Abraham, Isaac and Jacob believed in the Lord God. They hoped in his promises; hence they "looked forward to a city founded, designed and built by God" (Heb 11:10).

Jesus Is Our Hope

But the fullness of human hope is shown in the revelation made to the chosen people of God through the Word made flesh, Jesus Christ. He comes to give us hope against fatalism, the belief that after human death there is no other life eternal. He comes to drive out from our lives all despair and fear that come from the loss of hope in God's mercy and love. In despair we assume our sins are mightier than God's love and forgiveness.

He also delivers us from a false hope built on presumption. Such presumption believes in God's constancy of love and forgiveness, but, like a spoiled child, refuses to see the need to respond as true faith requires to God's overtures of love.

More positively, Jesus Christ comes to reveal to us by his teachings and above all, by his acting out from his nature as one with the Father, the infinite love the heavenly Father has for each of us, his children. This is revealed in his self-emptying of the last drop of water and blood when his heart was pierced on the cross.

We have no way to know the Father's love for us and to receive his forgiveness save through the Son, who reveals to us the Father (Jn 14:9). This is the unbelievable Good News that Jesus Christ "died for us so that, alive or dead, we should still live united to him" (1 Thes 5:10). Jesus is our hope and in him we can trust because we believe he is the perfect image of the heavenly Father made human for us.

Jesus spoke these hopeful words to his disciples on the eve of his self-emptying death for love of all of us: "As the Father has loved me, so I have loved you. Remain in my love" (Jn 15:9). Jesus is telling us that he has the same infinite, outpouring, emptying love for us that the Father has for him. We must abide in that love.

And we do abide in that love when we trust in God's unchanging love in all details of our lives. We trust, therefore, that he will forgive us all our sins, now and at the hour of our death. But what does it really mean that God forgives us our sins?

Forgive Us Our Trespasses

How many times we have prayed the Our Father, the prayer Jesus has taught us to pray, as embracing the main elements of our relations toward God and neighbor! Does it mean, when we pray "forgive us our trespasses as we forgive those who trespass against us," that God will act toward us in a forgiving way only if we first do something, namely, forgive others who have offended us?

If we place God outside and depict him as we depict ourselves, we will never be able to trust in his forgiving power. Yet do not most Christians believe God waits for us to shape up before he ever loves us or answers our prayers? Do we not fashion him according to our image?

To trust absolutely in God's love we must firmly believe through God's revelation, especially in Jesus Christ, that God is love and goodness by his very nature (as we pointed out in Chapter 1). We do not have to ask God to love us. We cannot even ask why God has been absent in meeting our needs. The very nature of God as a community of self-emptying, loving persons within the Trinity is the very same nature of that trinitarian community, constantly self-emptying for us in an unconditional love that is being manifested in our lives at all times. The manifestations of God's goodness and loving care are unveiled in different circumstances at each moment of our lives. Yet God's nature is always and consistently to be unconditional love for all his children.

We cannot merit his love or receive it as a reward for what we first have done. We must trust because of God's revelation: "I have loved you with an everlasting love, so I am constant in my affection for you" (Jer 31:3). The love of God manifested in Jesus is God's free, unconditional love, first given to us, as John writes in his first epistle: "This is the love I mean: not our love for God, but God's love for us when he sent his Son to be the sacrifice that takes our sins away" (1 Jn 4:10).

God-Trinity is always invading and bombarding us at every moment with the self-giving of each unique Person, Father, Son and Holy Spirit, in each moment of our lives. We cannot earn this loving presence. We must surrender ourselves to God, who is always love.

Therefore, when we pray for God's forgiveness, we do not pray that God will do some action of forgiving us our sins that he has not already done in his constant love. It is *we* who must come into God's everlasting, merciful, forgiving love that is *always* present to us if we open up to become recipients of himself as gift of forgiving love. Only if we are touching God's love and being transformed by that love to be beautiful children of him, the source of all being, can we truly forgive all those who have trespassed against us.

Our prayer to God for his forgiveness and our prayer that we may forgive others who have hurt us are really our ongoing prayer of conversion to turn away from our sinfulness and turn toward God's forgiving love, always there and available, but only if we avail ourselves of it. As we turn in our need to accept God's forgiving love, we will also be transformed into a forgiving love by God's Spirit to forgive all others who have trespassed against us.

Do Not Judge Others

True forgiveness of God toward us is nothing less, from God's viewpoint, than his constant love as mercy, condescending to us in our miseries and sinfulness. His forgiveness is always present and active, if we only would repent and cry out for the grace of the Spirit to be converted and become like little children, foolish enough in God's wisdom to believe that God truly loves us and wishes to heal us of all that impedes a greater share in his fullness of life.

How sad to think of so many Christians believing through an intellectual assent that God really does forgive them because his love is ever constant and perfect, but never allowing themselves to be transformed by such an intellectual act of faith! It is only when the Spirit touches our heart and gives us deeper faith, hope and love that we can realize God cannot, humanly or divinely, love us more than his active, trinitarian presence dwelling within our very physical beings. God cannot give us more of himself. It is we who must wake up and receive of his fullness.

> You will with all the saints have strength to grasp the breadth and the length, the height and the depth; until, knowing the love of Christ, which is beyond all knowledge, you are filled with the utter fullness of God (Eph 3:18–19).

Such a conversion is a transformation away from our false self to begin to live as Jesus did, a reflection of the Trinity's love for us. This reception of God's forgiving love, when sincerely and humbly accepted by us, counteracts despair and presumption. It calls us in our transformed oneness with Christ to live with him in self-sacrificing love toward all others whom we encounter.

There we have a true test of whether God has forgiven our sins. We cannot partake in any mere external ritualism of making an act of contrition without a conversion of the heart, or of receiving, in a magical sense, the sacraments, especially the rite of reconciliation and the Eucharist, even though in such rituals and sacraments we indeed can encounter the risen Jesus in his full, forgiving love, which truly can take away our sins, if we really wish to amend our lives.

To enter into God's constant, forgiving love is also on our part to become children of the God we have received. It is to be transformed by God's merciful love, to be godly by our new birth through his Spirit, into authentic children of our heavenly Father. The degree of such a transformation is measured by how consistently we are forgiving of those who injure us. Loving our neighbors, especially our enemies, and forgiving them the injuries they have caused us, is the proof that we have become what God has always meant us to be: his children.

> But I say this to you: love your enemies and pray for those who persecute you; in this way you will be (children) of your Father in heaven (Mt 5:44–45).

Are you at this moment fearful and anxious as to whether your sins have been forgiven by God? If you can imagine yourself lying on your deathbed at this moment, breathing the last breath of your earthly life, would you trust in God's forgiveness of all your sins?

God's forgiveness from his side is assured to us. His forgiveness is his constant mercy extended always to us. This is the hope we have in God's nature as love coming to us in our miseries. This is the trust we have in Jesus Christ, who dies for us that we may attain a share in his glorious, eternal life with his Father through his Spirit.

Such trust in him is not passive on our part. It is an active receptivity to accept the Trinity's burning love for each of us and the entire universe and to cooperate in each moment in our continued transformation into authentically loving children of God. It is up to us in the power of the Spirit of the risen Jesus to put aside all selfishness that sows seeds of fears and anxieties, knowing God's perfect love has taken away our sins.

Only we can determine to live, no longer we ourselves, but to let Jesus Christ live in us. "Those who are in Christ Jesus are not condemned" (Rom 8:1). No sin of the past or present can haunt us with doubts or fears, for Jesus Christ has set us free by his Spirit.

St. Paul's statement about why we should no longer fear condemnation or unforgiveness of our sins beautifully summarizes the message of this chapter:

> After saying this, what can we add? With God on our side who can be against us? Since God did not spare his own Son, but gave him up to benefit us all, we may be certain, after such a gift, that he will not refuse anything he can give. Could anyone excuse those that God has chosen? When God acquits, could anyone condemn? Could Christ Jesus? No! He not only died for us — he rose from the dead, and there at God's right hand he stands and pleads for us.
>
> Nothing therefore can come between us and the love of Christ, even if we are troubled or worried, or being persecuted, or lacking food or clothes, or being threatened or even attacked.... These are the trials through which we triumph, by the power of him who loved us.
>
> For I am certain of this: neither death nor life, no angel, no prince, nothing that exists, nothing still to come, not any power, or height or depth, nor any created thing, can ever come between us and the love of God made visible in Christ Jesus our Lord (Rom 8:31–39).

Prayer of Forgiveness

Heavenly Father, in awe and reverence I fall before your majesty, holiness, beauty and goodness. You are the snow-capped mountain on which the gazelle and the young stag joyfully leap and bound. I am a darkened desert valley in which there is no beauty, but what flashes as brilliant light from you into my nothingness.

O Father, your child is sad and filled with tears. I am frightened as I crouch in the depths of darkness and despair. Fears and anxious worries, like bats shearing wildly through a confining cave, beat my soul. The evil in my heart clutches around my throat. I gasp for your life-giving breath as my sinfulness covers me with the cloak of death.

There is no place to go but to cry out in my desperate search to look upon your face. My spirit, like parched earth, cries out to you, my heavenly Father, for your healing mercy, your forgiving love!

Send me your forgiving Voice, your Word made flesh, Jesus, my Savior, to speak in stillness deep as summer fields kept windless in the blazing sun of noon and silvered in the silence of the night, and yet as loud as thunder. May his Spirit come upon me as healing Love, that I may receive your forgiveness.

My past sins, my omissions, my hurting others in my self-centeredness, rise up to haunt me. With the psalmist, I desperately cry out to you:

> From the depths I call to you, Yahweh,
> Lord, listen to my cry for help!
> Listen compassionately
>   to my pleading!
>
> If you never overlooked our sins, Yahweh,
> Lord, could anyone survive?
> But you do forgive us:
>   and for that we revere you.
>
> I wait for Yahweh, my soul waits for him,
>   I rely on his promise,
>   my soul relies on the Lord
>   more than a watchman on the coming of dawn
> (Ps 130:1–6).

Lord, Jesus Christ, let me hear you command me as you did the entombed Lazarus, "Come out!" I pray earnestly that your forgiving love will unbind me and set me free. I believe, for me you have died. Looking into your blood-covered face as you hung dying on the cross, I sob for your forgiveness. As the soft morning dawn gently lifts the darkness from the face of the earth to let the sun burst into being with full radiance, so let the light of the Father's love softly fall upon my broken spirit to drive away the darkness of despair and abandonment.

I know in my brokenness I cannot buy or merit your forgiveness of my many sins. I believe you are Love by your nature, always present with warm love, ever covering me as rays of summer sun drive out all coldness of limb.

I need only to walk out of my coldness and darkness into your loving presence to receive your new life. Gather up into your mighty arms my past sins and, like fire touching sun-dried straw in the fields, burn up into vanishing smoke my sinfulness and leave me purified by your forgiving love.

Lord Jesus, you are the Father's mercy in my miseries. In you I trust that I am forgiven all my sins. In you I believe I can begin a new life. In you there is no longer any condemnation. Your love has set me free!

Loving Father, let me hear you say to your prodigal child, who asks your forgiveness, the beautiful and consoling words Jesus spoke in the gospel parable: "We are going to have a feast, a celebration, because this child of mine was dead and has come back to life; he was lost and is found" (Lk 15:23–24).

Jesus! Abba! I trust in you because you truly love me!

CHAPTER 5

Trusting God in the Present Moment

Have you honestly and often thanked God that he has placed you in his loving providence into this beautiful world at the present time with all its exciting enrichment and fantastic discoveries? The discoveries through nuclear physics, astronomy and space technology simply stagger our minds as to what awaits us as we explore God's gifts of the universe. Nuclear physicists take our breath away and dizzy our minds with their ability to release, in the splitting of the atom, energies capable of transforming or obliterating our entire world.

Such power and magnitude locked inside of creation, no longer conceived as a static moment as the Book of Genesis might lead us to believe, should give us a more dynamic experience of God as Creator in process of creating this universe — but with the cooperation of human beings. It should unfold to us a God who in his humility has freely invited, and does so in each moment of our human existence, each of us human beings to open ourselves to his loving, dynamic, creative power, which unfolds before our eyes in the context of each moment.

The "Newtonian" God was static, objectified and not close to us in his loving care. In such a theism this perfect and immutable God relates to his world-creation through absolute laws embedded in nature. Modern scientists no longer oppose religion but furnish us with a dynamic view of matter and of God. God interacts in a synergistic cooperation with his human children to direct the further creation of this world into one of harmony and peace. Niels Bohr, the famous Danish physicist, has expressed this change in our thinking:

> The great extension of our experience in recent years has brought to light the insufficiency of our simple mechanical conceptions and, as a consequence, has shaken the

foundation on which the customary interpretation of observation was based (*Atomic Physics and the Description of Nature*).

A New World

Such scientists allow us to move into an exciting, exploding world in which God is creatively evolving the *this-ness* of each creature, working with his human creatures in the process of building this world. Through Einstein's theory of relativity, it should become easier for us to believe that God sees this world as a unity. All parts are meant to be coordinated into a whole, into a dancing harmony. All creatures, through the creative inventiveness and cooperation of us human beings, working through our free choices with God, are meant to be interrelated in a harmonious wholeness. Each part, even physical evils, has its proper place within the universe. Each creature depends on and gives support to all the others in one great whole, in one great body, all of which is being created in and through God's Word.

The Dignity of Human Beings

Such a view of a world, in flux and yet under the loving concern and active, creative power of the triune God, must change our attitudes about our relationship toward God. Before such an amazing display of power, energy and beauty in the created world, in the heavens and on the earth, we might think we human beings are of little concern to the omnipotent God.

Yet God's revelation of himself as found in scripture should now give us greater trust in his loving mercy and in his humility to so love us as to give us his only-begotten Son. The most lowly, most abject, most uneducated, most ignorant, most degenerate human being is loved infinitely more by God than he loves all the galaxies in his night sky.

We must trust that God is meeting us in each moment and humbly asking us to cooperate to make this a more beautiful universe in which to live and work. God has elected us to be the consciousness, the love-spark, that can ignite the whole and lead the entire universe with God's graceful power into a unity of diversity. We have the power to "enspirit" the matter of the universe, not only into ourselves, but into a unity of one body — that of the total Christ in whom "were created all things in heaven and on earth" (Col 1:16).

God calls us in each moment to meet him and co-create the world:

> God blessed them, saying to them, "Be fruitful, multiply, fill the earth and conquer it. Be masters of the fish of the sea, the birds of heaven and all living animals on the earth" (Gn 1:28).

We are overwhelmed by the great dignity God has given us in creating us according to his own image and likeness:

> I look up at your heavens, made by your fingers,
> at the moon and stars you set in place —
> ah, what is man that you should spare a thought for him,
> the son of man that you should care for him?

> Yet you have made him little less than a god,
> you have crowned him with glory and splendor,
> made him lord over the work of your hands,
> set all things under his feet,...

> Yahweh, our Lord,
> how great your name throughout the earth! (Ps 8:3-6,9).

Called to Be Participators in Creation

In 1905 Albert Einstein prepared the way for the discoveries of modern nuclear physics with his theory of relativity and "slew a beautiful theory with an ugly fact," in the words of T. H. Huxley. Einstein proved that Newton's absolute space can no longer be considered as an independent absolute. Space and time are interrelated and form a fourth-dimensional continuum, which physicists today, using Einstein's term, call space-time, to show that all reality is relational.

Einstein showed, therefore, that man is not a detached observer, but a participator. We must see ourselves in the space-time continuum, participating in events that have an impact on each participant. We never observe a fixed world outside of ourselves. The light of the sun takes eight minutes to reach us on the earth. We never see the sun's light, therefore, objectively in a static, fixed way, but always as it was eight minutes ago. We see the nearest star as it existed four years ago, and with powerful telescopes, we see galaxies as they existed millions of years ago!

Process Theology

Today many theologians, through better scriptural studies and influenced by nuclear physics, are seeking better ways to express God's love and active concern for his created world than the traditional theistic expressions. Dr. D. D. Williams, one of the Protestant process thinkers, following the insights of Alfred North Whitehead, describes God in interrelationships as co-creating with human beings, as they cooperate in their free choices:

> The biblical God acts in a history where men have freedom which they can misuse. He is at work in time, and it is just this which the theological tradition, conditioned by neoplatonic metaphysics, has never been able to encompass (*The Spirit and the Forms of Love*, p. 107).

In such a process-view the world is seen as a dynamic reality rather than a static reality. Human nature is not immutable and independent of the entire universe and God himself. The world is seen as an interrelating society of "occasions," in which no isolation is possible. The richly interconnected, interrelated series of events present God as vitally involved in the flux of everything, as the divine Orderer and Harmonizer of all things.

Whitehead distinguishes in God his true, unchanging essence as God's *primordial nature*. In this nature God sees all possibilities from all eternity in one perfect vision. God in his nature cannot be acted upon, or suffer any relationship from outside creatures. In God's *consequent nature* Whitehead presents us with God actually involved in vital relationships with all his creatures. When God freely decides to create a material world and creates man and woman as the consciousness of the universe, he also freely consents to enter into vital relationships with man and woman and, through them, with all of his creatures. What happens to the world is of concern to God.

God responds concretely in each "event" to bring about his *telos*, or original end or goal, for which he decreed to create his universe. God is not the process, but is a conscious community of divine Persons ever going forth in loving, self-giving activities in and through his creation.

Human Free Will

In such a process of interrelationships among God and human beings and all of creation God freely wills to invite us human beings, whom he has created in order to share intimately in his triune life, to cooperate in loving oneness as we, together with God, bring forth the universe in its fullness.

God so respects our human freedom, since he freely has created us according to his very own image and likeness, that he never forces us to any one preferred line of action. God is a power to do all things, yet it would be contradictory to his own willed decree to give us free will and then to violate it by coercing us to do his will. God actuates possibilities by drawing us into the orbit of his beauty, truth and love. He gently persuades, like a loving father toward his children, as he offers to us various possibilities to fulfill the destiny of his children. We are allowed to enter into a cooperative venture as he lures us with his gentle attractions of tender love.

God, from all eternity, is absolutely *necessary*. All other creatures are contingent and dependent upon him. He is absolute transcendence, perfectly omnipotent and omniscient. He is always independent of his creatures. Yet clearly from revelation in scripture, God shares his freedom and creativity with his human children.

As our loving Father, God wishes in each event of each moment that we freely respond to his love, especially as it is manifested by his only-begotten Son, Jesus Christ, and as it dwells within us as the triune community of the eternal God. God's providence contains a special involving work of God to accept lovingly and respectfully the free choices we human beings make. He "adjusts" himself to those choices in order to draw out what will be "saved" and conducive to God's ultimate end in his creation.

Whitehead seeks to describe this working of God to save in every event what can in some way work unto good for those who love the Lord:

> The image — and it is but an image — the image under which this operative growth of God's nature is best conceived, is that of a tender care that nothing be lost. The consequent nature of God is his judgment on the world. He saves the world as it passes into the immediacy of his own life. It is the judgment of a tenderness which loses nothing that can be saved. It is also the judgment of a wisdom which uses what in the temporal world is mere wreckage (*Process and Reality*, p. 525).

Jesus lived his earthly life in a way that he summarized in the words: "My Father goes on working, and so do I" (Jn 5:17). As we have seen in Chapter 2, Jesus strove to surrender in trusting obedience to the Father's will in each moment. He found his Father unveiling himself as Love, pouring himself completely into the Son's being and calling him into his Sonship in each moment of each event. He does nothing at any time of himself, but only in the Father's power and love in order to please him.

Jesus' earthly life was an arduous pilgrimage to the Father, carried out in silent, trusting, surrendering love. "Tempted in every way that we are, though he is without sin" (Heb 4:15). Nonetheless, his journey to the right hand of the Father, where he reigns today in glory, was a constant struggle with his human desires in order to bring them into perfect conformity to the Father's will, the one thing he had come to do: "To do your will, O my God, is my delight" (Ps 40:9 NAB).

As Jesus grew daily from childhood through adolescence to young adulthood, he learned to turn more inwardly to find his Father at the center of his being. There in the depths of his heart he, who was "nearest to the Father's heart" (Jn 1:18), breathed, smiled, laughed and cried in that holy presence. He learned to trust in the Father's goodness and holiness in every event of his earthly life.

From the pages of the gospels we see how Jesus moved about doing good wherever he went. He actively ministered to others by preaching God's Word of love and bringing healing and hope to the oppressed and the maimed. In the midst of many activities, fatiguing journeys on foot, attacks by opposing religious leaders, and even rejection by those whom he had lovingly served, Jesus shows us a consistent picture of one who lovingly trusted his heavenly Father in all details of his daily life.

Jesus acquired, through such childlike trust in his Father, a different evaluation of what was occurring in his everyday life. What most other human beings would consider as pleasant or unpleasant became for him the "occasion" or opportunity to trust in his Father's active love working unto good in all things.

Especially in his final sufferings and death on the cross Jesus learned trust as he sought to do, not his will, but that of his Father. Such trustful abandonment to whatever the Father was asking him to do brought Jesus deep peace. In his death he passed over to a new life of glory. In his resurrectional presence through his Spirit, he can now abide in us, members of his body, the church. He who in his humanity silently listened to God as he spoke his Word in him and trusted that all would work unto good now speaks from the depths of his disciples' hearts, if we Christians only would trust in the Father's working in each event of our daily lives.

God's Uncreated Energies

In order, therefore, that we too might in every event surrender in childlike trust to the workings of the heavenly Father through his Son, Jesus Christ, in their Spirit of Love, we must change our view of a God that is detached and immutable to a God that is truly Love by nature. We must put on the reality Jesus lived in and operate in all things out of that living reality.

Love, in order to exist in human beings or in God, must always be loving, always pouring itself out from its own abundance, always giving of itself to others. Tied to the mysterious makeup of God as an I that is also a *We*, is God's bursting forth from within his own perfect, circular, loving self-containment to love us so that we might accept his love and become happy in sharing his own family life, that of the Trinity.

As the great mystics of early Eastern Christianity taught, God in his essence cannot be comprehended as he really is by our human intellects. No human being has ever seen God and lived. Yet, scripture and these early mystical theologians show us that God lovingly and freely wishes to share his very own being with us. God actively "goes forth" out of the Trinity, yet as a Trinity of individual persons, Father, Son and Holy Spirit, in self-giving to us by means of what the Fathers called his uncreated energies of love.

Accepting the doctrine of God's energies, by which he gives himself to us through his loving actions, will allow us to trust in God's loving presence. These energies or actions are not things God does to us, or on our behalf. God's energetic actions are God as he, from his one essence, dynamically gives himself to us. Through God's energies we actually do make contact with the living Trinity. If God is truly love by nature, he must, therefore, want to give us, not merely created graces as things, but himself as gift. The energies are really God as Persons in interrelationships toward us giving himself as he is personalized in his energies.

God Is Grace

Thus from God's viewpoint there is no action of his that can be termed natural or supernatural. God is, at all times of our lives in every moment, giving himself in real, self-giving relationships as uncreated energies of love. Grace, therefore, is God as individual Persons, Father, Son and Spirit, giving themselves in loving actions to us and all of God's creation.

If we are eating, drinking, sleeping or working, God is powerfully present and working for us in loving activities unto our eternal happiness. All is sacred, as we are bombarded by the Trinity's gifting of itself to us. But we must have eyes of faith and a childlike trust to encounter God immanently inside of all of matter and acting in all events in his universe out of his infinite love for us.

The whole universe is bathed in the grace of God's divine energies. We can never be alone, separated from God. If we lack this faith and trust in God, we live in sin, which is disbelief (in the Johannine sense of sin) in God's loving nature. But, it is God's providential working in all things unto our happiness that is revealed in the sacrament of the present moment.

A Theology of the Event

If God is "inside" the stuff of each moment, he must be effecting what these signs are symbols of: his great self-giving toward us. J. P. de Caussade in his classical work *Self-Abandonment to Divine Providence* gives us the very suggestive phrase, "The sacrament of the present moment." Sacraments are visible signs made up of material things and gestures along with words that lead Christians into an effective encounter with Jesus Christ, who brings about through his Spirit what the signs signify.

Through our faith that God is creatively present in each moment we can, therefore, believe that he is in an analogous way effecting a sacramental self-giving thus and bringing us into a greater union with him.

In the context of our Christian lives the Holy Spirit gives us faith to see the Trinity operating in each moment. We can, thus, reverence and adore his sacred presence. As we surrender to his loving activity, God's Spirit reveals to us that what Jesus effects in the primal eucharistic gift of himself in the sacrifice of his life on the cross for us, and in the sacrament of love, is also being accomplished by the three persons of the Trinity, Father, Son and Holy Spirit, on our behalf in each moment.

In the faith, hope and love with which we encounter the Trinity operating in self-giving love on our behalf in each moment, we can joyfully relinquish control over our lives, plans, desires for this moment. We can stretch out in total abandonment as we yield to the Trinity's dynamic, loving activity in this *now* event.

God Found in the Event

By the power of the Holy Spirit's gifts of faith, hope and love, we are able to move into a new knowledge beyond all human knowledge to "see" God as touching us in all moments and drawing us into a more intimate union with him. Faith rips off the false masks and created worlds we have been fashioning out of our false securities where God is considered far from us. And how we fear to trust in his active love in each event! Such faith brings forth hope and trust that leads us into a love that becomes a

return of self-giving on our part for the continued self-giving of
God on our behalf.

The *event*, therefore, is whatever is happening to us at any
given moment. It comes from the Latin verb *evenire*, which means
"to come out of." It places the emphasis on the dynamism of
God's providential concern. By *providence* we refer to the superior
dealings or actions of the Creator with his creation, the wisdom,
omnipotence and goodness with which he maintains and governs
in time this distinct reality according to the counsel of his own
will. This is rooted in God's free choice to create the world, and
especially us human beings, for a purpose.

God's providence has God working to effect the goal for
which he has created us. Providence guarantees and confirms the
work of creation, for we realize that no creature could be if God
did not choose continually to confirm and guarantee and main-
tain it in being.

Creation and God working in the event of the now moment
to create according to his eternal plan are identical. In creation it
is a matter of the establishment, the incomparable beginning of
the relationship between Creator and creature. Providence looks
rather to the continuation of creation and history in a series of
different, but comparable, moments. Providence looks to God's
reciprocal relationship with his creatures to advance the fulfillment of his plan.

The *event* is the moment in history in which God is always
acting out of his love and goodness to bring about his intended
goal. He has been actively concerned and caring for us human
beings in every moment. But we are usually asleep to his loving
activities; we are unaware of his active love. We must go "into"
the event with faith, hope and love, rooted in God's revealed
Word. God "comes out" of the event, the moment in history. We
go to meet him in his loving, active concern for us. We go there to
discover him as energetic love and to work with him in faith,
hope and love.

Importance of the Present Moment

There is in reality only this given, present moment in which
we can open up to God's meeting us in history and his desire to

bring us into a sharing in his divine life and happiness. Yet, because of our isolation and ignorance of our inner beauty as loved already by God so infinitely in Jesus Christ, we take things into our own hands. We interpret a given event that impinges itself upon us in any historical moment according to our false ego and not according to our true self in Jesus Christ.

Blaise Pascal comments on how we live under fear of the past or the future and thus lose the only contact we have with God's reality:

> We never hold ourselves to the present time. We antici-
> pate the future as coming too slowly in order to hasten its
> advent. Or we recall the past in order to stop its passage
> too rapidly. Too imprudently we err in times which are
> not ours and we do not think of what only is in our power,
> what truly does belong to us.

> So in vain do we hunger for those things which are no
> more and, thus, we let fly away, without batting an
> eyelash, the only thing that exists. This is the present
> which ordinarily wounds us. We hide it from view be-
> cause it afflicts us. And, if it is pleasing to us, we regret
> seeing it pass (*Pensees*, No. 172).

It is in this present moment that we find God's love present-ing itself in a new incarnation. Jesus is being revealed as our Savior. The heavenly Father is inviting us to experience him as our true Father, who really does love us. The Holy Spirit hovers over us in the seeming chaos of the present moment in order to allow God's love to make us into a new creation in Christ.

Is it not true that we become bound and enslaved to the past and the future out of fear, while we blithely ignore the present that alone can bring God's healing to the past hurts, loneliness and sinfulness? By opening ourselves wholly to the present moment in complete trust in God's creative presence, we move into the real future "that no eye has seen and no ear has heard, things beyond the mind of man, all that God has prepared for those who love him" (1 Cor 2:9).

Illumined by Faith

How exciting to realize these things prepared for us are not the static, eternal ideas predetermined by a God who is totally detached from our material world! Rather, our faith in the presence of God in this given event calls us into a great adventure. We are called into God's creative, loving energies to co-create with him out of the raw-stuff of each moment the only *real* world there is, namely, the world of living and loving in his holy will.

It is not enough for us to open ourselves to God's gift to us of the present moment. By faith we "see" God, get in touch with his loving activities and then work with him to effect a transformation to something better. Faith illumines us in a freeing way to see God inside of the present moment. But there is a freeing by faith also from ourselves and the limitations that we place upon ourselves and upon God through our fears and selfish desires. We can do all things in him who strengthens us.

Our Free Cooperation

Faith does not lead us into presumption, but into a true assessment of each situation and what we can do with God's help to change matters according to God's will. True gentleness and meekness in childlike trust in God's power and love are rooted in humility, seeing reality through faith according to God's eyes. We can turn the other cheek to our enemies, but God would want us also to work diligently to transform them into our brothers and sisters by our love and prayerful intercession.

There is an Amish proverb that says: When you ask God for potatoes, don't forget to pick up the hoe. We trust that God will provide for what we are to eat and put on, but that means someone has to prepare the food and put the clothing on us. God will provide us with health, but it may mean an operation and a stay in the hospital. We can pray and trust God will provide us with a job, but his will directs us also to knock on doors and seek employment. Parents must love their children, but they must also make efforts to discipline and correct them. Part of God's order is that we do all that depends on us.

St. Ignatius of Loyola in his *Spiritual Exercises* wisely exhorts us:

Rely on God by doing everything as though the success depended entirely on you and not on God. And, moreover, while using all of your efforts to succeed in the given matter, do not count on those, but only as if God alone must do it all and you nothing.

The theology of the "event" centers on our free-will cooperation with God's loving activities. True love is only possible with our human, free cooperation with God's will. St. Augustine, who preached so eloquently the harmonious interaction of grace and human cooperation in loving faith and trust, wrote: "He that created thee without thy knowledge will not save thee without thy consent" (*Sermon*, 109, 13).

God's Beyondness

As we embrace each event we open to the loving presence of God. We trust in that loving presence as being one with the unchanging revelation in Christ Jesus of God's undying, infinite love for each of us. Thus, each event is charged with God's presence as uncreated energies of love. But this presence always contains something of a mystery that is *beyond* and *unreachable* by our own power or merits.

We are challenged by God's Spirit to take a risk that God will really be *there* with his omnipotence, working out of infinite love for us unto our eternal happiness. Hope allows us to go beyond our own controlled reality, as we open in a risk to seek the hidden, loving God. R. Troisfontaine writes:

In the light of God calling me to personal communion, my whole life is as a test to me, in each of its circumstances; it always includes a temptation and a stake.... Salvation is to find in every reality its relation to the beyond. The test is that which has a beyond (*De L'Existence a l'Etre: La Philosophie de Gabriel Marcel*, vol. 2, p. 48).

In each moment we are called to risk and to live in trust by staking everything on God's loving fidelity to us. We cannot fathom how God will be present in each given event. Still we hope and trust in his loving presence. We allow him to possess us

totally in each moment. And we can do so only because the Holy
Spirit *inspires* us. He breathes into us a trust in God's goodness and
perfect holiness. Our hope is in him, even as we look at our own
poverty and inability to understand or even cope with the given
situation.

Like his loving children, which we really are, we are at peace
with our complete surrender to him. We no longer nervously
want to control ourselves, or even God, or other persons around
us. A gentle openness to each event and all persons involved
becomes an habitual attitude on our part.

Trust Leads to Abandoning Love

By trusting in God's active love in each moment, we learn to
see all persons, ourselves included, all other creatures and all
events that touch our lives, in God's *Logos*. This glorious Word
made flesh, Jesus Christ, risen from the dead, empowers us
through the release of his Spirit to contemplate the Trinity in all
things and all things in the Trinity.

The strange paradox that we experience in each moment is
that the more we trust in God's self-emptying love for us in each
event, the more he does not abandon us. He reveals himself as a
loving Father in ways that cannot be expressed in human words.
Such childlike trust leads us to a state of loving abandonment that
is the end of our lives. We have truly become what God the
Father called us from all eternity in his Son, Jesus Christ, through
his Spirit of love to become.

Charles de Foucauld formulates the following prayer that is
not only the result of trust in God working in each moment, but is
also the goal of our eternal life:

> Father, I abandon myself into your hands. Do with me
> what you will. And for whatever you may do, I thank you.
> I am ready for all. I accept all. Let only your will be done
> in me and in all your creatures. I wish no more than this,
> O Lord. Into your hands I commend my life. I offer it to
> you with all the love of my heart. For I love you, God, and
> so need to give myself, to surrender myself into your
> hands without reserve, and with boundless confidence,
> for you are my Father.

CHAPTER 6

Trusting in Human Love

You may smile at how naive I was as I share this personal experience. In 1957, as I was making my eight-day retreat in preparation for ordination to the priesthood in the Russian-Byzantine Rite, I was carried away by God's generosity and love for me. In prayer, I offered him three things:

1. I promised God I would always be a *poor* priest (not a *pathetic* one, or a "poor" excuse for a priest!). I would live as poor people live. I would seek castoff clothing to wear; sleep on a board, instead of a comfortable mattress; and so on.

2. I would always seek the more difficult assignments, those that bring great humiliations and humility. And, oh yes, God, if possible, please grant me the great grace of dying physically a cruel martyrdom.

3. God, I promise never to kiss a woman!

After finishing a doctorate and returning to New York to begin work after 18 years of studies that fairly successfully kept me out of touch with a great deal of God's "real" world, I had a lot of catching up to do! In my apostolic work of teaching, counseling, preaching retreats, hearing confessions, I found myself presenting Christianity as a religion of love. Yet I felt uncomfortable, for I had been taught to *love* and *serve* God, but only to *serve* other human persons. To truly love any "particular friend" was considered a distraction and great danger; such a friendship might take me away from my love of God.

I struggled with ideas acquired in modern psychology, especially concerning personalism, insights from a holistic spirituality of the early Eastern Christian mystics, Yoga, and the modern thinker, Pierre Teilhard de Chardin. The charismatic renewal brought me a freedom and joy in expressing what I saw now clearly as the essence of Christianity: "My dear people, let us love

one another since love comes from God and everyone who loves
is begotten by God and knows God" (1 Jn 4:7).

Back to God I went. "About that poverty: that still stands,
even though the board isn't getting any softer! And OK, also,
about that martyrdom, if *you* still think it's a good idea! But God,
about kissing women, we've got to talk!"

Searching for Love

You and I move like some stalking animal in a feverish hunt
for happiness. It takes some time in our human journey before we
realize that everything other than God — money, pleasures,
travel, food, sex, fame — will never bring peace and joy to that
burning longing within us for a happiness that would never bring
us boredom, that would be imperishable, that would last forever.

After some limited experiences in life we soon learn that
there can be no real happiness, except through love. God, who
"is love" (1 Jn 4:8), has made us out of his trinitarian love to share
intimately in his community of love as his very own children,
regenerated by God's Spirit. But God also communicates to us the
experience that he is love when his uncreated energies of love are
experienced by us in unselfish giving and receiving love from
other human beings. They, in their unselfish love for us, and our
love returned unselfishly to them, become the *place* where God
again incarnates his great love for us. "No one has ever seen God;
but as long as we love one another God will live in us and his love
will be complete in us" (1 Jn 4:12).

The I Is the Child of the We

The loving touch of another human being is the beginning of
our discovery that God is truly love. Each moment someone loves
us unselfishly in hope that we are more beautiful in their eyes than
we consider ourselves to be, we begin to grow a bit into the true
self that God knows us to be. Each time we respond by returning
the gift of ourselves in love to the other, we are set free from the
greatest enemy in the world, our selfish ego, and we know that
freedom and love can never be separated.

Without God, we cannot love. Without the other in human
love, we cannot show our love. In both the process necessitates a

true dying, a letting go of our narcissistic absorption, as though we constitute the only center of reality. This dying is life-giving by our being birthed into our true selves, created by God to be one in Christ, by loving others and receiving their love with him as he has loved us.

Gabriel Marcel, a noted Catholic philosopher, succinctly expressed this birthing of our true identity through a loving community when he wrote: "The *I* is the child of the *We*" (*Journal*, p. 62). When we have the courage, through God's Spirit of love, to confront the seeming death to our false securities and to make the passover leap through trust in the other, we open ourselves to a new birth of consciousness of the uniqueness in our personhood.

True love is life which decentralizes itself, which changes its center. When we love, our interior defenses, self-consciousness and pretenses fall along with the barriers that separate us from another. We are opened to the vulnerabilities of ourselves and to the other. True uniqueness as a person is a creation of love, because in love there is renewal and rebirth. One who loves me discloses me to myself. In the beautiful and deeply meaningful words of e. e. cummings:

> It's not two ones are two,
> but two are halves of one (*Poem XVI*).

Trinity: Persons in Ecstasy

The above statement — which brings into the true mystery that which is closed to our mere human reasoning powers, but open to those who humbly surrender to self-sacrificing love — is at the heart of all human loves. It is at the heart of God himself as a community of love. The Greek Fathers were fond of describing the interpersonal relations of Father to Son through the Holy Spirit as a process of moving toward the other in personalized Love, the Spirit in *ekstasis*. In Greek this means an ecstasy, but not in our limited Western understanding of the word. *Ekstasis* is a standing outside of one's habitual control by which a subject, seemingly with one's rational powers, controls an objective world through the mind. It is to break down all "walls" that separate two persons.

If God is love by nature, then, within the heart of all reality God is a community of three persons mutually moving toward each other in loving self-giving. In the ecstasy of "standing outside" of themselves and becoming available through the gift of love to live for one another, the Persons of the Trinity — Father, Son and Spirit — come to know themselves as unique, distinct Persons, who are united in passionate, self-emptying love. In joyful surrender to one another, the Father and the Son discover their uniqueness in their oneness through the hidden, emptying Spirit of Love.

Since we have been made according to God's own image and likeness, it follows that we are called to model our lives upon the divine community, the Trinity. In addition, the Good News Jesus makes possible, through his death and resurrection and outpouring of his Holy Spirit, empowers us by the indwelling Trinity to live in such "ecstatic" love toward others.

Called to Intimacy

When we love another with deep intimacy and commitment, measured by the three characteristics of intimacy — *availability*, *mutuality* and *self-sacrifice* — God is again made flesh in that love. We are called to be open and available to all human beings, made by our one Father to be brothers and sisters, members of the Body of Christ, and united into a oneness through the Spirit of love.

But from our own human experiences we clearly know that we cannot be equally present in self-sacrificing love to all persons whom we meet. We lack the psychic power, the time and possibilities of becoming intimate with all human beings. We need primal communities, bases of loving identity to which we go as to a "home" to become re-created, re-birthed into higher levels of consciousness of our true selves as unique persons and from which we go out to love others, but in a lesser intimacy, a lesser total self-giving.

Christian Marriage

Jesus, through his teachings and those continued through the teaching authority in the church down through the centuries, presents marriage as sacred and life-giving. It is a sacrament in which a husband and wife are prayerfully, in deep faith, hope and love, to meet Jesus Christ, their Savior, who transforms by grace their sincere, loving desires into one body as he is one with his church.

A logical analysis of marriage will never succeed in presenting its true essence. Because marriage brings together the uncreated energies of God, loving and giving himself to the married couple, it remains always a mystery that must be approached in a prayerful reverence. It is the basis of all human communities of love. It is the ideal of all Christian love, since it is modeled on the very love of God, incarnated and manifested to us in Jesus dying for love of his spouse, the church. This is the ideal St. Paul holds out to all married persons, but also to those who are single, or living in the celibate state as recognized by a life of vows:

> Husbands should love their wives just as Christ loved the Church and sacrificed himself for her to make her holy. He made her clean by washing her in water with a form of words, so that when he took her to himself she would be glorious, with no speck or wrinkle or anything like that, but holy and faultless. In the same way, husbands must love their wives as they love their own bodies; for a man to love his wife is for him to love himself. A man never hates his own body, but he feeds it and looks after it; and that is the way Christ treats the Church, because it is his body — and we are its living parts.... This mystery has many implications; but I am saying it applies to Christ and the Church. To sum up; you too, each one of you, must love his wife as he loves himself; and let every wife respect her husband (Eph 5:25–33).

This is what Pope John Paul II called having the "nuptial mindset" of Jesus. In being called to be married, or single, or celibate, all of us share in a basic vocation given by God to all human beings, and that is to achieve "nuptial" intimacy. What does this mean?

The ideal in Christian marriage demonstrates this type of intimacy. The married man and woman are called to self-abandoned love, not only during the moments of symbolically positing the essence of the sacrament as total self-giving on the body, soul and spiritual levels during conjugal intercourse, but this self-surrender is to be lived out in true self-giving, beyond any rational limits, to each other in the details of daily living.

In orgasmic ecstasy, for a few moments, two loving mates experience totally an abandoning of self-control or "reasonableness." They forget who they are, and where they are, for those moments. It is an exchange of vulnerabilities, a melting into a communion of oneness that frees each person to discover a new sense of identity and inner beauty as unique. This is the love Teilhard de Chardin defines as "love differentiates as it unites" (*Phenomenon of Man*, pp. 264–67).

Nuptial Intimacy

What are the characteristics of this nuptial intimacy that should form the basis for all true, loving relationships that are life-giving? Seeing these, we will be in a better position to understand the need of trust in such human love.

We are born into finiteness through limitations of time, space, our own individuality, our human nature. We are born "into sin," which is a basic bias in favor of oneself in isolation and independence from others. The remedy is to come into an adult maturation of our human nature, to move out of isolation and independence into a sharing of our lives with others in true love, idealized in marriage. It is a communion, through total availability on body, soul and spirit levels; a mutuality of equality within sexual differences that brings about an *I–Thou* relationship through continued self-sacrifice on behalf of the happiness of the other. It is a community of love, which allows two different persons to become one without ceasing at the same time to be two, unique, free, self-sacrificing persons.

True love is a fundamental option that only we can choose for ourselves. It is our unique way of becoming truly human and thus attaining our fulfillment and meaningfulness in loving relations with God and the human persons whom we love intimately.

To love with the nuptial mindset of Jesus toward us is to give undivided attention to another person. It is to give of our very life by entering into that person's world. It is to touch the core of that person's uniqueness and, in doing so, to discover the core of our own uniqueness. We put aside our own control, our preferences and narcissistic centering upon our needs.

True Love

Thus we can distinguish true love from infatuation or the popular idea of what superficial persons might call love. It is not basically and solely a feeling, a sensual feeling, a gratification of sexual appetites. Love is something we choose, or decide to do, because it results in a self-sacrifice of oneself in favor of the other. It is to be a gift of one's uniqueness to the other. Therefore, as in all marriages and all loving friendships between those who are single or celibate, love is a personal choice freely made. Such love does not have to *feel* good all the time. Its essence consists in willing personal goodness and happiness and fulfillment for the other.

Love cannot have an "angle." God does not love us in order to supply a need that is lacking to his perfection. God freely loves because he freely wills to do so out of his abundant goodness. If we were to love someone for some reason, it would not be true love. If we make love subservient to anything other than purely to live for the good of the other, it is a prostitution and in no way can be called true love.

In true love we find all our happiness and fulfillment in seeking the good of the other. We learn to love another, not *as if*, but as his or her *other self*. Such intimacy destroys selfishness, while selfishness destroys such true love. This is why Christianity unceasingly preaches, and hopefully practices, the necessity of loving others as Jesus has loved us.

To live in such communion with another, and others, we must respect the integrity and inner dignity of the other persons as persons with an individuality all their own. They can never be conceived as mere objects by one who truly loves. By putting ourselves at the service of the happiness of the other, whom we love, we also touch the very intimacy of the Trinity toward each of us.

To Love Is to Suffer

We have been created out of God's love and that of our parents to become beautiful, unique people, empowered to beget new loves and in such new loves to discover more and more our uniqueness in freedom to give ourselves to ever-wider circles of friends. Yet the most life-giving experience for us human beings is to discover God in the very loving of another. We also experience that this often can bring with it the greatest pain. Think of all the brokenness brought into this world through marriage relationships and other intimate friendships, and how often such brokenness is passed on to future generations! Why is it so difficult to love others intimately without bringing suffering to ourselves and to others?

As we learn, both in union with God and friend, when we take the risk of opening ourselves to the other at the core of our being, we begin to experience fears and doubts. It becomes more difficult to trust the other; we often become riddled with suspicions about the authentic love of the other for us. We discover new areas unknown to us before.

In marriage one of the devastating effects of selfishness, which destroys true love, is the tendency of a husband or wife to control the other as though he or she were a mere possession, an object meant for petty exploitation. True marital love is total, self-giving, permanent until death and exclusive. As Christ directs his love exclusively toward his church, so each partner must realize, by God's grace operating in their sacrament of matrimony, that their love of total surrender to each other cannot be shared with anyone else in the same manner of complete self-giving to each other.

A true test of mature love in marriage is the ability of each partner to trust the other and to allow the loved one freedom to develop his or her talents without interference, but rather with loving support and encouragement. Each partner needs a certain amount of physical, psychic and spiritual space in order to develop. Marriage should never stifle the unique growth of the partners, but enhance and support it.

Danger Signs

In friendships among those who are single there are danger signs that rise up along the way to deeper intimacy. Which way, Lord? How should we express, enflesh our love for one another? What should we say, and how should we say it? When are you leading, Lord, by your Spirit of love and when, perhaps, are we deluded by passion, unregulated and rationalized?

The true destroyer of childlike trust in God's guidance may lie in the confrontation of unredeemed, hidden areas within the unconscious, never before suspected of being there and exerting any influence. Perhaps in the past we experienced the lack of physical affection shown to us by a loving friend. We begin to "need" the other to supply the needs that come out of our unconscious.

Demands for sensitivity and fidelity not known before are made in proportion as we accept the gift of the other. Like the Israelites, we become tired of obeying God in the deep mystery of faith, hope and love, and we wish to return to the "fleshpots" of Egypt or to build a false, golden calf as our god of worship.

In true love, as we have pointed out, the self can no longer be the center of focus as we humbly and honestly seek to live and serve God in the uniqueness of the other. Noises from within rise up out of our inborn selfishness to destroy our listening to God's Word operating in the life and needs of the other. The demands may be too great; the sacrifices, far too many.

The desert of so many unknown and mysterious factors challenges us to trust more in God and our beloved. Life seemed so simple earlier when we were in control and were receiving so much from the other. But now the call to be silent in the desert of our inner poverty and to listen in more trusting love to the needs of the other threatens our security. The familiar, our long-time control over the situation, is no longer a luxury we can selfishly enjoy.

Bittersweet

To reach a oneness with another in God's love is to taste a bit of heaven already on earth. But it is also to taste a bit of hell in terms of personal suffering. What agony to let go and not possess or manipulate the other! Any separation from the one loved is as though we were cut into two parts now distant, and we long for the joy of coming into the presence of the other. And yet, when we come together, how tempting to want the other to measure up to our expectations and needs.

So many of our sufferings in loving another intimately come especially from the undeveloped trust and hope we have in the other. The one loved has not yet experienced himself or herself as good, noble or beautiful. Yet we are expected, by God's call, to truly love that person by preceding such love, or deeper growth in that love, with greater hope and trust.

Selfishness can cause us to lose the sense of wonder and mystery, poetry, spontaneity and the going-beyond to live in the tremulous hope of the not-yet. Such a lack of hope in the other makes true love impossible. It is a return into isolation. Even worse, it is a foretaste of the essence of hell.

Martin Buber in *I and Thou* gives us a Hasidic parable of what true love consists:

> (He) sat among peasants in a village inn and listened to their conversation. Then he heard how one asked the other, "Do you love me?" And the latter answered, "Now, of course, I love you very much." But the first regarded him sadly and reproached him for such words: "How can you say you love me? Do you know, then, my faults?" And then the other fell silent, and silent they sat facing each other, for there was nothing more to say. He who truly loves, knows, from the depths of his identity with the other, from the root ground of the other's being, he knows where his friend is wanting. This alone is love (p. 248).

St. Paul characterizes true love this way:

> Love is always patient and kind; it is never jealous; love is never boastful or conceited; it is never rude or selfish; it does not take offence, and is not resentful. Love takes no pleasure in other people's sins but delights in the truth; it is always ready to excuse, to trust, to hope, and to endure whatever comes (1 Cor 13:4–7).

Trust in God and in the Beloved

We can see that the degree of trust we manifest in our relationships with God, and the hope we have that God's Holy Spirit can integrate our brokenness and our many faults that tend toward pride and selfishness, also measures the degree of trust we manifest toward a loved one in his or her frailty and even habits of selfishness. It is not that we love another in spite of his or her weaknesses, but it is the deep trust and hope in the basic beauty that lies in the other that allows us to pass over to true love. We believe that God is the source of all life, and what is impossible for us to accomplish is possible with God.

The greatest sufferings in my Christian life have come in my sincere attempts to be love to some few intimate friends. To promise God not to kiss a woman was easy to achieve by my own power. But to search through my brokenness and through the brokenness found in the loved friend, and there to develop trust in God and trust in the other's inner dignity and beauty, *that* is a crucifixion! And that is precisely the call Christ gives to every Christian who seriously wishes to follow him.

> If anyone wants to be a follower of mine, let him renounce himself and take up his cross and follow me. For anyone who wants to save his life will lose it; but anyone who loses his life for my sake, and for the sake of the gospel, will save it (Mk 8:34–35).

Trustful Abandonment to God's Spirit

If the Holy Spirit is leading us in true love in all our human relationships, he brings us to an inner freedom, which results from dying to our aggressive false ego, in order to be open in gentle receptivity to encounter God in the other. This freedom shows itself in a humility that is able to sublimate our pride and self-containment and express in look and word that our greatest privilege and joy is to live for the happiness of the other and, in that, we find our happiness and true being.

Such freedom allows us to give ourselves in hopeful trust that others will accept us. Our total availability, according to our state of life and responsibilities to God and others, opens us up to be refused and wounded by others. But because the gentleness of God's Spirit is continually transforming our isolated ego, we are able even to transform such hurts. The cross of Jesus can be deeply experienced in what God has meant to be one of the most beautiful of human experiences.

And yet the peace and joy that we experience in surrendering to the Spirit of love allow us to swing free from rejected love to seek humbly in deeper trust to be led by the Spirit to offer ourselves to others. They too may reject us, use us and hurt us, yet we entrust ourselves to God's Spirit. How easy it is to make abstract acts of trust in God and in the basic goodness of a person loved by us! But true trust is developed only in circumstances that call us to a choice to act trustingly, or not, in this concrete, loving friendship.

We know from past experiences of love-relationships that the end of our lives is to offer, as Jesus did, ourselves to others in love. There is no other way to human fulfillment and happiness. Yet such love passes through the purifying fires of living in ever-deepening trust in God and others. The pain and risk of letting go and surrendering in trust cannot compare to the healing joy of finding in another human being the presence of God, loving both of us and calling us into a greater union with him and with each other.

Our abandonment to God's love is measured concretely by how ready we are to trust the Spirit in another, who offers us the privilege of loving him or her, and letting go of our isolation to become a trusting community in God's love. At the heart of heaven is purgatory, the therapy necessary to purify our true love by self-surrendering trust. At the heart of true love is the agony of passing through death-to-narcissism and entering into the painful agony of trusting in the actual context of building a community of self-sacrificing, godly children of the triune community of God himself.

CHAPTER 7

Trust in Time of Suffering

From all times in the history of the human race people have asked the same question and will continue to do so, perhaps even more so in our modern times: If God is a good and all-powerful God and really loves us, why does he cause or permit evil and its concomitant suffering, especially to the innocent? You and I, in the throes of our personal sufferings, have no doubt posed this question to God.

German poet Rainer Marie Rilke in "To Live Everything" offers deep insight to Christians who seek a rational answer to so perplexing a problem:

> Be patient toward all that is unsolved in your heart.....
> Try to love the questions themselves....
> Do not now seek the answers,
> which cannot be given because
> you would not be able to live them.
> And the point is,
> to live everything.
> Live the questions now.
> Perhaps you will then,
> gradually,
> without noticing it,
> live along some distant day
> into the answers.

This chapter is not meant to give an exhaustive study of deductive and inductive ways, even from scripture, to explain why suffering exists in our world. Its aim is to go beyond rational answers. Let us become, as Gabriel Marcel enjoins us to do, a question to ourselves.

The Christian is not to seek answers from Jesus, for he came not to give answers but to become the question about suffering. When the Word of God leapt out of the triune community of love and in peaceful silence came into a world of sin and death, evil and sufferings, he did not come to take away all evil and sufferings. He came to take upon himself all our sins and sufferings. He suffered as you and I do, not to be an answer to our problems about evil and sufferings, but to become the Way whereby we could rise in a transformation from sufferings with Christ to a sharing, even now, with him in glory.

Knowledge Beyond Human Understanding

It is quite human to reflect on the quality of our lives and to seek to understand the choices presented to us to lead meaningful lives or isolated ones. Down the centuries, in all religions and cultures, men and women have undergone sufferings and witnessed evils perpetrated, especially against the most helpless and innocent. It is natural to probe the reason or cause for such sufferings.

Some religions and cultures have seen sufferings and evils as inevitable. Death is a liberation, therefore, a blessing whereby human beings can escape from them. Some, like the Stoics, have sought to master suffering through a grim asceticism, which rendered them insensitive to pain, but also to others.

Others have rebelled against sufferings and evils, like Ivan in Dostoyevsky's *The Brothers Karamazov*. They reason that a good God could not exist before such overpowering evils. Revolt becomes, for them, the power to fulfill themselves.

Other religions encourage the faithful passively to resign and endure such sufferings since there will be a reward in a future heavenly existence.

The Jews in the Old Testament held two predominant attitudes toward sufferings. We find the typical, popular attitude given by the three friends of Job. Sufferings befell an individual because of personal sins committed against the laws of God. Job insists that he has not sinned and brings a turning point to Jewish thinking as he moves to a humble surrendering to God's love and wisdom.

The world of faith in a loving God presents, not a rational answer for the presence of sufferings in all human lives, but a faith and trust in God's goodness and power to draw out of such darkness new creative manifestations of his glory. The Book of

Job presents us with Job's response to the problem of evil and sufferings. There can be no logical answer, since divine wisdom and power are beyond any human power to understand. Faith must carry on even when understanding fails.

> I know that you are all-powerful:
>   what you conceive, you can perform.
> I am the man who obscured your designs
>   with my empty-headed words.
> I have been holding forth on matters I cannot
>   understand,
>   on marvels beyond me and my knowledge (Jb 42:2-3).

Beyond all questions God might well be answering: "Trust in me and my love for you. What is impossible for you to understand is possible for me to draw much good from. All things, even sufferings, work unto good to those who love and trust in me."

Jesus — The Way

Jesus did not come to give us answers to our many problems, especially the one about why we have to suffer so much in this life. He clearly distinguished between 1) evils that God could not create and still be true to his nature as loving us, his children; and 2) sufferings, which he taught we must accept when they come into our lives, and also crosses that we must willingly embrace, as he did — crosses that result from obeying his command to love him and others as he loved us.

We are to study his actions, as recorded in the New Testament, and to reflect on his teachings, especially his parables, in order to move into the hidden world of faith, which alone can encounter mystery beyond all human understanding, and to respond in childlike trust to God's call to deeper union with the risen Lord.

Jesus in the Gospels

In the gospels we often find Jesus being confronted with the problem of evil and suffering. Representative of his approach to such a problem is the incident of the Pharisees asking Jesus to explain why the man was born blind. The Pharisees offered the common belief among the Jews at that time: "Rabbi, who sinned,

this man or his parents, for him to have been born blind?"
(Jn 9:2).

The answer that Jesus gives is one of faith, not logic. "He was
born blind so that the works of God might be displayed in him"
(Jn 9:3). The man is healed. His very blindness is turned into a
manifestation of Christ as the light of the world and the one who
initiates people into the kingdom of God, away from the power of
sin and death of the kingdom of darkness.

Suffering, in the teaching of Jesus, is never the result of a
moral evil that transgresses God's holy will. Two men looked out
prison bars. One saw mud and the other saw stars. Suffering is a
pain that can be turned into good or evil according to the way we
perceive it. St. Peter in his first epistle teaches us how to
accept sufferings as means to encounter the victory of the risen
Lord Jesus.

> Blessed be God the Father of our Lord Jesus Christ, who
> in his great mercy has given us a new birth as his sons, by
> raising Jesus Christ from the dead, so that we have a sure
> hope and the promise of an inheritance that can never be
> spoilt or soiled and never fade away, because it is being
> kept for you in the heavens. Through your faith, God's
> power will guard you until the salvation which has been
> prepared is revealed at the end of time. This is a cause of
> great joy for you, even though you may for a short time
> have to bear being plagued by all sorts of trials; so that,
> when Jesus Christ is revealed, your faith will have been
> tested and proved like gold — only it is more precious
> than gold, which is corruptible even though it bears
> testing by fire — and then you will have praise and glory
> and honor (1 Pt 1:3–8).

This Christian faith, through trusting hope in the power of
the risen Lord Jesus, can transform by his Spirit what seemingly
appears as failure, evil and negativity into life-giving, eternal joy.
As St. Paul writes:

> By faith we are judged righteous and at peace with God,
> since it is by faith and through Jesus that we have entered
> this state of grace in which we can boast about looking

forward to God's glory. But this is not all we can boast about; we can boast about our sufferings. These sufferings bring patience, as we know, and patience brings perseverance, and perseverance brings hope, and this hope is not deceptive, because the love of God has been poured into our hearts by the Holy Spirit which has been given us (Rom 5:1–5).

Jesus and Suffering

What was Jesus' attitude toward suffering and evil? Like his Jewish ancestors he wrestled, not so much in an intellectual struggle about the *why* of evil and suffering, but with the forces of evil that permeated far beyond any individual human being, what St. Paul called "the principalities and the powers." Realistically, Jesus encountered evil as a cancerous virus pervading all of human society, its institutions and the structures of the world.

Jesus encounters evil wherever he finds it, and his strategy is to invite his listeners to accept not the mere hope of some eternal happiness in the life to come, but himself as the Way to greater, unending life. He insisted — with those who gave him a hearing — that the only answer to the problem of suffering stemming from evils, seen and unseen, is to follow him into life and live the way he lived his life unto greater glory.

Like a warrior leaping into the battle Jesus approached the problem of evil and the concomitant sufferings as a warfare against inimical powers. Sin is more for Jesus than individuals' free and deliberate choices against God's commands. The mystery of evil has invaded deeply within the human unconscious and also throughout the cosmic strata. It was precisely this collective mystery of evil that Jesus encountered during his human existence on earth and conquered by his inner oneness with his all-holy Father and Spirit of self-emptying love.

He became the Suffering Servant of Yahweh, foretold by Deutero-Isaiah, a man similar to us and "familiar with suffering" (Is 53:3). Gabriel Marcel says that our souls are made or unmade by the quality of our response to suffering. We can see how Jesus, in the personal encounter with evil and the sufferings that came to him from various sources, became, in a gradual process of struggling in faith, hope and love with such evil, transformed by the very darkness into the eternal, glorious light that he was from all eternity.

Jesus encountered our doubts and weaknesses. He daily encounters us in our Emmaus journey to chide us:

> You foolish (people)! So slow to believe the full message of the prophets! Was it not ordained that the Christ should suffer and so enter into his glory? (Lk 24:25–26).

Jesus, the Suffering Servant of Yahweh

Whatever Jesus asks of his disciples, he himself did in his earthly life. When he washed the feet of his disciples, he summarized who he was. He was *Ebed Yahweh*, God's servant, suffering for his people. Although evil forces heaped upon him much suffering, he sought to bear the sufferings of those who came to him for help as well.

And the reason he could move to a higher dimension of viewing evil and sufferings was that he was vitally conscious that everything he did came from his Father. He lived only to please the Father and bring him glory. Over and over he confessed that he was nothing, while his Father was all.

Jesus reveals an inner consciousness of his ultimate worth and meaning as a human being who derives all meaningfulness from his complete dependence upon the Father. There is no vanity or self-seeking in his words or actions. His primal motivation is to serve the wishes of his heavenly Father. He lives in his loving presence, as he becomes more and more surrendering in each moment to the working of his Father in his life. "My Father goes on working, and so do I" (Jn 5:17). "As the Father has loved me, so I have loved you" (Jn 15:9).

Embracing Sufferings Unto Death

Jesus and his early disciples were aware that his whole mission in life was to serve the Father's will. But it became progressively clearer to him that his service to the Father was to be a service on behalf of God's people. He lived in human form the truth that love is always active, self-emptying, and always ready to bear all sufferings, even death itself, to show that love for others.

That service, in God's eternal plan, was to be pushed to such self-forgetting that Jesus would become a free gift of himself on behalf of the human race. He would literally and freely give himself to die for each of us. His attitude toward evil and suffering can never be separated from his consciousness that he was to become the perfect image in human form of how much the heavenly Father loves his children, even unto death.

Jesus recognized that to make concrete his service to humanity he, the Good Shepherd, would lay down his life for all human beings. As Suffering Servant, Jesus fulfilled the prophecies of Deutero-Isaiah by being a victim on our behalf. He was not a victim of circumstances turned over to the wiles of those who persecuted him. To fulfill the divine plan of propitiation for the sins of humanity he somehow bore the sins of the world and took them away: "Look, there is the lamb of God that takes away the sin of the world" (Jn 1:29).

Love Is Suffering Self-Emptying

St. Paul presents a hymn, well-known to the Christians of the first century, as the way and the reason why Jesus emptied himself on our behalf by his death on the cross. And he introduces this hymn of divine love with these words: "In your minds you must be the same as Christ Jesus:"

> His state was divine,
> yet he did not cling
> to his equality with God
> but emptied himself
> to assume the condition of a slave,
> and became as men are;
> and being as all men are,
> he was humbler yet,
> even to accepting death,
> death on a cross.
> But God raised him high
> and gave him the name
> which is above all other names
> so that *all beings*
> in the heavens, on earth and in the underworld,

should bend the knee at the name of Jesus
and that every tongue should acclaim
Jesus Christ as Lord,
to the glory of God the Father (Phil 2:6–11).

Jesus' attitude before sufferings and even death itself is seen as
an act of faith, hope and love; he turned in complete submission
and obedience to do His Father's will. He disregarded the shame-
fulness of the cross, enduring it for love of us. For this reason the
Father exalted him, giving him the name of Lord of the universe,
allowing him to be called by the name no man could utter:
Yahweh, truly God!

Creative Suffering

I often ask in prayer, "But, God, why death on the cross?" It
is similar to our queries about why we should have to suffer in our
personal, earthly lives and why the innocent ones of this world
suffer. Both questions cannot be understood intellectually; they
can be met only by a blind resignation before a mighty God whose
justice demands repayment for sins. There is surely more that the
Word of God reveals to us in deep contemplation of Christ's
sufferings, which only his Holy Spirit can reveal, far beyond the
reach of our puny human minds.

From the pages of the gospels we see that Jesus strove throughout his human life, especially in his public life, not only to do
perfectly what was revealed to him to be the clear commands of
his Father, but also to do the wishes of his Father, revealed by the
Holy Spirit.

The extreme sufferings of Jesus, physically, psychically and
spiritually, can never be understood logically. Just as our human
love knows various degrees of acting out in generosity the love we
have for another, depending on how much love we have experienced from God and other human beings, so Jesus, in intimate
union with the Father, must have received progressively deeper
and deeper assurances of the Father's self-emptying love for him.

As Jesus experienced in prayerful communion his Father's
perfect love for him, he grew in his sensitivity to what love was
asking by way of a self-oblation. He wished to go beyond the
boundaries imposed by justice or even by the delicate whisperings

of what the Father wished of him in any given moment. This is creative suffering. It is what keeps love alive. It is fire touching dry wood and making it turn into fire also.

We can, perhaps, now begin to see a shadowy outline, not of an answer to why we need to suffer in our lives, but of the way that Jesus chose on our behalf. And he invites us to come to him to learn how he suffered so that in his Spirit of love we too might learn to suffer all things creatively.

Jesus, loved by the Father infinitely, was being driven in his human consciousness, not by any obligation of justice, but by the consuming desire to take his life into his own hands and freely give it back to his beloved Father. In emptying himself by his free choices to suffer more and more, Jesus was becoming the expressed image of his heavenly Father in human form.

He had said, "To have seen me is to have seen the Father" (Jn 14:9). Jesus, in utter freedom and spontaneity, especially in his passion and death on the cross, was improvising before the entire world how he suffers in human form to mirror to us how great the Father's self-emptying love for each of us is.

Light in Darkness

The Suffering Servant of Yahweh, Jesus Christ, true God and true man, now becomes better understood by us, not through our human logic, but with purified hearts through the Spirit, who enlightens us to this knowledge that is beyond all human understanding. There is light in the darkness of Jesus' *kenosis* or self-emptying love.

It is not just that he *had* to suffer and die in order to save us from eternal death. Throughout his whole life Jesus freely chose, when there were possibilities, to descend into the heart of human beings who were lost to God's love. He chooses to descend into the suffering, dying heart of humanity. He freely wishes to become the poorest of the poor, the loneliest of all abandoned human beings. His love for the Father burns so strongly within him that he goes into the dregs of humanity and desires to become a part of the lowest of the lowliest.

As the prophet Isaiah foretold, he wills to be crushed as a worm beneath the cruel heel of this world, which crushes so many other men and women. He freely wills, by his human choice, to taste every ingredient in the bitter chalice that the world, in which the mystery of evil rules, can press to human lips.

He did not ignore human anguish but took it upon himself. He did not come to eradicate from our earthly lives all our sufferings and evils. He came to walk the path of all human sufferings. He not only images the passionate love the heavenly Father has for us by dying in human form out of love for us, but he freely consents to take upon himself our sins and infirmities to suffer with us and for us.

Deutero-Isaiah had prophesied that the coming Messiah would associate with us in our sins and sufferings:

> Without beauty, without majesty (we saw him),
> no looks to attract our eyes;
> a thing despised and rejected by men,
> a man of sorrows and familiar with suffering,...
>
> And yet ours were the sufferings he bore,
> ours the sorrows he carried.
> But we, we thought of him as someone punished,
> struck by God, and brought low.
> Yet he was pierced through for our faults,
> crushed for our sins.
> On him lies a punishment that brings us peace,
> and through his wounds we are healed (Is 53:2–5).

Flesh of Sin

In becoming human Jesus came under the Law. Taking on our human nature and born as we are, Jesus Christ, the Son of God made man, has also associated and taken upon himself our "flesh of sin." St. Paul clearly teaches that Jesus became incarnate to take our sins upon himself so that we could live by our higher nature. "God dealt with sin by sending his own Son in a body as physical as any sinful body, and in that body God condemned sin. He did this in order that the Law's just demands might be satisfied in us, who behave not as our unspiritual nature, but as the Spirit dictates" (Rom 8:3–4).

He, the just and the righteous One in whom there is no sin, stands in our sinful and unrighteous place.

St. Paul writes that Jesus justified us by his blood (Rom 5:9). The blood, for Paul and for us, should symbolize the suffering and death of Jesus on our behalf. In giving us Jesus as our propitiation-victim, God shows us how great is his love for us and his desire to share his very own life forever unto our perfect happiness.

As we contemplate prayerfully Christ's suffering and death, freely taken upon himself for our sakes, we see what it costs God to be righteous and true to his nature in his hatred for sin. He wishes to destroy sin by his Son incarnating all sinfulness of humanity. The Father shows his righteous disdain for self-centeredness, the root of all sin and moral evil. We begin to understand only in Christ, suffering on the cross unto his death, what sin is and how God, by his very nature, must resist it. Only in Jesus can we see God's full judgment on sin. Only in him can sin be taken away by the blood of the Lamb of God.

We no longer need fear God's judgment upon us for our sins. We need only fear that we do not believe in God's righteousness, which Jesus won for us. And we openly show to God and the world around us whether we are righteous and living in God's righteousness by living in the power of the Holy Spirit to produce the fruit of the Spirit, and no longer living in guilt and sin.

True Children of God

As living members of Jesus' body, we live by our uniqueness in Jesus; we obey his commandments to bring forth works of love that flow out of our new, regenerated nature. Freed by Christ from slavery to sin, we Christians become slaves to righteousness and to God, as Paul writes in Romans (6:15–23). We live in the continued experience that we are children of God, even now.

Jesus gives to us who have been born into the sin of our ancestors (the "sin of the world") the capability of living now in the grace of regenerated children of God. Through his suffering and death on the cross Jesus laid his hands on the roots of evil in human history and uprooted them. By becoming human as we are, he also assumed the sins of us all.

He does not give us a logical answer for our sufferings and those of all other human beings the world over. Nor does he promise to put an end to all evils and sufferings in this temporal world of ours. The gospel of Jesus is an invitation to us to believe as he did in a God of unconditional love, even amid our most extreme sufferings and the evils in and around us.

Pope John Paul II explains how Jesus takes away our sins by suffering:

> This suffering may be called vicarious, but it is first of all redemptive. The Man of Sorrows of this prophecy (Is 53:2–6) is truly "the Lamb of God who takes away the sins of the world" (Jn 1:29). Sins are taken away by his suffering because he alone, as the only-begotten Son, could take them upon himself and accept them with that love for the Father which overcomes the evil inherent in every sin. In fact, he reduces this evil to nothing in what may be called the human race, and he fills that space with goodness (*The Christian Meaning of Human Suffering*, No.17).

Jesus, Our Redeemer

The Son of the heavenly Father, of one substance with him, by the incarnation is able to suffer and die as a man. His sufferings are truly human, just as ours are. He "has been tempted in every way that we are, though he is without sin" (Heb 4:15). Yet Jesus who suffers and truly dies, is also the only-begotten Son.

> He alone, the Only-begotten, is competent to assume the whole weight of evil to be found in the sin of man; in every actual sin and in the universal sin corresponding to the circumstances of the historical existence of the human race on earth (*The Christian Meaning of Suffering*, No.17).

This is what transformed St. Paul: He experienced in his sufferings his sinfulness, and yet, in the resurrectional presence of Jesus the Lord dwelling within him, he found the strength to bear all sufferings that came to him.

> I have been crucified with Christ, and I live now not with my own life but with the life of Christ who lives in me. The life I now live in this body I live in faith: faith in the

Son of God who loved me and who sacrificed himself for my sake (Gal 2:20–21).

Thus we Christians believe and trust in Jesus Christ as our sole Redeemer and Liberator from sin and death. All human beings on the face of the earth have to bear many sufferings during their earthly sojourn. Yet Christians are graced to live in the mystery of faith in Jesus Christ, which transforms our very sufferings into a more intense sharing in the Trinity's eternal life. By the Holy Spirit's gifts of faith, hope and love, we can rise from what seems to be a disastrous, meaningless, even irrational suffering to embrace a new oneness with the risen Lord Jesus.

Faith is the midwife that assists us in emerging out of a dark cocoon of fear, doubt and ignorance as a newborn butterfly. Boring, monotonous events, even those of little or great suffering, can be consecrated by faith, hope and love into a *felix culpa*, a happy fault, leading from death to new levels of oneness with God and other human beings in love.

Such trying moments can become true participations in the resurrected life of Jesus Christ. In the very moment of consecrating our sufferings to God with Jesus, we already enter into a new sharing in his glory. As we abandon ourselves in loving surrender, we experience a new insertion into the life of Christ.

Importance of Sufferings for New Life

Jesus described the process of dying that is at the heart of accepting all sufferings with faith:

If anyone wants to be a follower of mine, let him renounce himself and take up his cross and follow me. For anyone who wants to save his life will lose it; but anyone who loses his life for my sake, and for the sake of the gospel, will save it (Mk 8:34–35; cf. Mt 10:38–39; 16:24–25; Lk 9:23–24; 14:27).

He insisted that the grain of wheat had to fall to the ground and die or else it remained only a grain. Only the dying would release the great potential of bringing forth new life. Only by living out our baptism, or passover from slavery into the trials of the desert of our heart, can we enter into the New Jerusalem, a sharing even now in God's life.

Sufferings, trials and tribulations are occasions for us to move beyond our own self-centered views of events surrounding us and become open to a faith-vision that only the Holy Spirit can infuse into the meek and humble of heart. We should pray daily:

> Teach me, O God, not to torture myself, not to make a martyr out of myself through stifling reflection, but rather teach me to breathe deeply in faith (*The Prayers of Kierkegaard*, ed. Perry D. Lefevre, p. 36).

Interiorizing Our Faith

The first stage of transforming our sufferings into stepping-stones to greater union with Christ is, in the words of the early Fathers of the desert, "to push the mind down into the heart." It is to enter into the "inner closet" that Jesus spoke about when he instructed his disciples how they were to pray in his Holy Spirit (Mt 6:6). This is a call to move away from our carnal-mindedness in order to enter into a transcendental presence to the indwelling Trinity. It is the place of the *heart* wherein we are to meet the risen Jesus, who reveals through his Spirit's faith that these sufferings at hand can truly work to good as "God co-operates with all those who love him" (Rom 8:28).

Yet how difficult this is to accomplish! We dread entering into our innermost selves. We fear we might just have to trust *only* in God and destroy all the idols that we have constructed in our minds of a God who can never even be given a name.

> The longest journey
> Is the journey inward
> Of him who has chosen his destiny
> Who has started his quest
> For the source of his being
> (Dag Hammarskjold, *Markings*, p. 58).

We are so reluctant to take those first steps into ourselves. The eyes that guide us through the labyrinthine darknesses can only be God's gift of faith. Only in inward silence, which sufferings invite us to embrace, can we hear God speak new meaningfulness in our sufferings. Such inner solitude, where we learn to leave the outside, flattering, pampering world of the senses and illusions, comes about only if we have the courage to taste our inner poverty.

This is the second value of sufferings. Sufferings force us to ask with urgency, "Who am I?" In asking this question, we are forced in our brokenness and sinfulness, our "zero-ness" of any power to bear with meaningfulness such seemingly illogical things as sufferings and evils, including our own sinfulness, to confront who Jesus Christ really is for us. Faith becomes a response to his invitation to suffer with him in order even now to enter into a union with him in living in his glorified, resurrectional life.

It is to know experientially through the Spirit's knowledge by faith what our personal sinfulness means, especially in terms of spurning, in the folly of stupid arrogance, the infinite love of God given to us through Jesus Christ who has died for us. It is to confront our inauthentic selves, covered by the hard shell of our self-containment or pride. We weep and mourn for our blindness, which leads us to the third value of sufferings: By consecrating through faith our sufferings as we sublimate them and live them in faith and childlike trust in the power of the risen Lord, we enter into a deeper union with Christ. We put on his mind.

Praise to the Lord

The sign of our emerging into a new level in Jesus before our loving Father through their mutual Holy Spirit is our readiness to praise God in all circumstances. We readily praise and thank God in prosperity when we happily receive from God health, riches or, at least, all the temporal things we are in need of: honors, friendships, successes in our undertakings. When such blessings come our way we readily hear Joel's words, "Sons of Zion, be glad, rejoice in Yahweh your God" (Jl 2:23).

But the true Christian learns through the Holy Spirit's infusion of faith, hope and love how to praise God in all seasons, under all circumstances. Praise is what flows from the depths of our being as we surrender lovingly to God, who is in all things loving us and showering upon us the gift of himself in whatever happens to us. With Hannah, we too can pray:

> My heart exults in Yahweh,
> my horn is exalted in my God,
> my mouth derides my foes,
> for I rejoice in your power of saving.
>
> There is none as holy as Yahweh,...
> no rock like our God (1 Sm 2:1-2).

Archbishop Oscar Romero of San Salvador was martyred on 24 March 1980. He gave his life for his faith in God and his love for his people, who were oppressed by the ruling powers in his country. His faith in the strength of Jesus suffering in him allowed him to move from mere speech to action. He abandoned all security and lived in constant risk as he involved himself more and more in the sufferings and oppressions of the landless poor.

Knowing that his stands against the rich were moving him toward a violent death, he spoke in one of his last sermons:

> I have tried to sow hope, to maintain hope among the people. There is a liberating Christ who has the strength to save us. I try to give my people this hope.... If I am killed, I will rise in the Salvadoran people.

With Job we too can say in our sufferings, "Let him kill me if he will; I have no other hope than to justify my conduct in his eyes" (Jb 13:15). Paul and Silas prayed and sang praises to God from their prison cell. We too can also raise our hands, even when sufferings bow them down to the earth, and pray, "We give thanks to God and the Father of our Lord Jesus Christ."

Our ability to rejoice and give praise to God in all prosperity and in all sufferings depends on our childlike faith in God's great love for us especially as manifested in Christ Jesus' sufferings, freely accepted out of love for us. Adversities purify our loving praise so that we praise God always solely because he is good and holy. Adversities allow us to humble ourselves before God that he may raise us up to a new union of love with him. How beautifully this is expressed in St. Peter's first epistle:

> Bow down, then, before the power of God now, and he will raise you up on the appointed day; *unload all your worries on to him*, since he is looking after you (1 Pt 5:6–7).

Let All Things Praise the Lord

God's loving presence is unveiling himself and calling us to a return of love in a faith response in the context of every event of every moment. Such events embrace all happenings, to which we can react in several ways, summarized by St. Paul as from a "carnal mind." We limit God's inbreaking love by interpreting the event according to our own center of reference. We find pleasure in certain circumstances and wish more of it. Other events bring us suffering and pain, and we want to avoid such moments. We seek to throw off such burdens as soon as possible. Suffering to us is a seeming evil to be avoided like a plague.

But by faith we can move beyond the surface and appearances of the event to touch the loving hand of the heavenly Father, who arranges all things sweetly through his providential care for us, and to praise him in all events. For such Christians, as we should humbly aspire to be, all things truly serve to glorify God. The weather of this day, regardless of how it upsets our plans, can become a point of praising God. How difficult it is to join the three young men in the book of Daniel to praise God in the frost and cold!

> All things the Lord has made, bless the Lord:
> give glory and eternal praise to him....
> Cold and heat! ... Frost and cold! ...
> Ice and snow! bless the Lord (Dn 3:57,67,69,70).

We have already mentioned the distinction theologians make between physical and moral evils. Physical evils are all those found in the temporal order of nature such as sickness, infirmities, physical poverty, famine, pestilence, earthquakes, wars, floods, droughts, freezing cold, blazing hot weather, and so on. The list is endless. The final and greatest physical evil that will touch all of us, eventually, is death.

And yet, whether we can discern what is willed or permitted by God, we must lovingly accept the merciful presence of God, even when we cannot understand what good could ever come out of such events.

Moral Evils

Theologians include in the category of moral evils all forms of sinfulness due to the free resistance of men and women to God's will. When we turn away in disobedience, we create moral evil, a thing God could never create; it separates us from the loving union with God. But our human sins have repercussions as well on the physical level of nature and in the lives of plants, animals and human beings, as we see today in the ecological problems caused chiefly by human greed.

Think of the destructive, physical evils released by a Hitler, a Stalin. Consider the explosion of atomic bombs over Hiroshima and Nagasaki, which destroyed hundreds of thousands of lives and has had untold repercussions in nature and the lives of future generations. Ponder the silent murder of millions of unborn, aborted babies in America and throughout the entire world.

We live in fear of nuclear destruction by the will of human beings. There was a time when we thought we could be concerned with our own sufferings and not those of others, especially in poorer, oppressed countries. Today we realize that we are all interconnected, not only for our survival, but also for mutual enrichment.

In an earlier age men and women could trust in God's providential care without much awareness of anything beyond a passive acceptance of a situation in trust. Today our universe presents the problem of sufferings and evils in a way that demands from us a different response.

A Global Village

Nuclear warfare; genocide; apartheid; global starvation; multinational corporations, which bleed and rape the resources of Third-World countries to make the poor poorer and the illiterate more illiterate; the unequal distribution of food stuffs, where so many countries have so much and others have so very little; all of these issues and many more should move us to a different understanding of evil and the purpose of suffering. Such sufferings should call us to become angry, as Jesus was wherever he encountered evil, either brought about by the invisible, satanic forces or by evil human beings.

Today Christ is calling us to fill up the sufferings of Christ in his body, the church, which is the leaven of what the whole world is called to become in Christ, its head. This way of redemptive suffering is the way of the cross, which Jesus invites all his disciples to carry with him. It is not sufficient, nor should it ever have been thought to have been sufficient in times past, for Christians only to question and wonder with the rest of the human race why God does not eradicate sufferings from the world, along with the evils that affect so many innocent persons. If the Master had to suffer and die in order to enter into glory, so we too must, but always out of love for others.

God evidently does not remove all sufferings from our lives just because we say prayers with this in mind. But he promises in Christ Jesus always to be with us unto the consummation of the world and to suffer with us. Jesus-risen makes it possible for us to experience the fundamental law of true love; namely, that the more we surrender in this life and in heaven to live in self-sacrificing love for another, the more we experience a new-founded sense of dying and rising, of possessing a new share in the glorious life of Jesus-risen.

C. S. Lewis in *The Problem of Pain* admirably captures this truth:

> As to its fellow-creatures, each soul, we suppose, will be eternally engaged in giving away to all the rest that which it receives. And, as to God, we must remember that the soul is but a hollow which God fills. Its union with God is, almost by definition, a continual self-abandonment, an opening, an unveiling, a surrender of itself.... We need not suppose that the necessity for something analogous to self-conquest will ever be ended, or that eternal life will not also be eternal dying. It is in this sense that, as there

may be pleasures in hell (God shield us from them), there may be something not at all unlike pains in heaven (God grant us soon to taste them).

God Disciplines Us Through Sufferings

Before we can grasp in loving trust the beauty of suffering in order to fill up the sufferings of Christ, let us see the oft-repeated reason found in the Old and New Testaments of why God not only permits evils and our own sins to happen, but why God also actively causes certain pains and sufferings to happen to us.

God can surely act on our behalf as he wishes and when he wishes, but we must believe from his revelation that, if he is love by nature, he always acts only out of love for us. Many of the evils and sufferings that we encounter come about either by God's permissive will in matters of moral evil (since God does not withdraw his sustaining presence as primary cause even in matters of sin), or by God's active working, but always to draw us closer to him, the ultimate source of all our happiness.

God, in scripture, says without any ambivalence, "I *am* the one *who reproves and disciplines all those he loves*" (Rv 3:19; Prv 3:12). Hebrews quotes the text from Proverbs 3:12 and most fully presents this common teaching about God's loving discipline in our regard:

> Suffering is part of your *training*; God is treating you as his *sons*. Has there ever been any *son* whose father did not *train* him? If you were not getting this training, as all of you are, then you would not be *sons* but bastards. Besides, we have all had our human fathers who punished us, and we respected them for it; we ought to be even more willing to submit ourselves to our spiritual Father, to be given life. Our human fathers were thinking of this short life when they punished us, and could only do what they thought best; but he does it all for our own good, so that we may share his own holiness. Of course, any punishment is most painful at the time, and far from pleasant; but later, in those on whom it has been used, it bears fruit in peace and goodness (Heb 12:7–11).

As gold is tested and purified in the fire of a furnace, so God puts his people to the test to make them worthy to be his chosen

ones. A beautiful image of the "shaping" of us by God is that of
the potter and the clay:

> Like clay in the hands of the potter
> to mold as it pleases him,
> so are men in the hands of their Maker
> to reward as he judges right (Sir 33:13).

Trusting Abandonment in Sufferings

The Old Testament offers us many outstanding examples of
faith and trusting abandonment. St. Paul appeals to Abraham
(Rom 4:18–25) as the model of faith and hope in God in adversities whose meaning escapes our human understanding. The
patriarch Joseph was faithful to God's guiding love when his
brothers threw him into a well and sold him as a slave to
Ishmaelite merchants for 20 pieces of silver (Gn 37:28). Tempted
by Potiphar's wife, he remained faithful to God, his strength in
times of trial. God used him, then, to save his people in a great
famine, but more importantly, to raise him up as a type of the
Messiah to come, Jesus.

King David, both in his sins and in his abandonment by his
friends and supporters, learned how to hope in Yahweh as the sole
true source of all strength and blessing (Ps 27:14). If we follow
David's trust in God, we too will hearken to his voice and meet
him in our troubles:

> I rescue all who cling to me,
> I protect whoever knows my name,
> I answer everyone who invokes me,
> I am with them when they are in trouble;
> I bring them safety and honor.
> I give them life, long and full,
> and show them how I can save (Ps 91:14–16).

But when God's word became flesh and dwelt among us, we
received the perfect revelation of abandoning ourselves to God in
any solicitude or anxiety. Besides, he pours out into our hearts his
Holy Spirit to enable us in all trials to trust in him, the Way to the
Father and to eternal life.

Jesus teaches us the reason we can abandon ourselves trustingly to God. We need only seek God's kingdom, letting him

have sovereign control in our lives, and then all temporalities will be given to us. "Your Father well knows you need them" (Lk 12:30).

Such abandonment can manifest itself in a variety of life-styles. St. Benedict Labre and St. Francis of Assisi surrendered to God's loving care in regard to food, clothing and shelter in a way different from an American businessman, nun or housewife. All Christians are to let go of any excessive worry and trust that in the circumstances of their life God will provide all they need. For parents, that may mean buying and keeping up a modest house, saving money for their children's education, taking out insurance against fire and theft. Abandonment and true poverty of spirit are possible in the context of using properly the riches God gives us, but as stewards, not as independent owners.

Such trust in getting rid of excessive worries and attachments to our possessions, because we believe in God's fatherly love and care for us, will move us to give to the needy whatever is beyond our moderate needs. And that alone will bring us much suffering as we war against those forces deep within us that want to have power by the possession of "things."

Trust in Sickness and in Death

Our health is a gift given us by God whereby we can grow in deep, personal relationships of love with others. We can be of loving service through our health. Health helps us to pray well, to travel and pursue many enriching human experiences. But trust in time of sickness can bring us to believe that the lack of health also can be a gift. If God permits sickness and even death to happen to us, or even wills it, he is really wishing us not sickness as an end, or suffering; rather, he is wishing us greater health, an opportunity to become purified to enter into a greater union with him, which will lead us into more total happiness to living as participators in God's very own life.

When the physical powers of our body, senses, intellectual acumen, memory, and so on begin to lessen, we have the graceful opportunity to experience our creatureliness and inner poverty before God. All other virtues — especially greater faith, hope and love toward God — develop if we utilize such sufferings to open to God as our sole strength.

Praying for Healing

Jesus has clearly taught us to ask anything of the Father and it would be granted as we believed. But this petition is to be asked in the name and according to the mind of Jesus. He prayed with childlike trust not to die on the cross, yet he used the very agony as he faced imminent death to surrender in loving trust to whatever his heavenly Father wished for him.

Before we pray for such healing, we must first discern whether we should ask for such and such. As we pray we enlarge our petition. If we believe a healing and longer life would be to God's greater glory, we must also open ourselves to receive from the Holy Spirit a deeper infusion of faith, hope and love.

From such a prayer of faith, individually prayed or in a group, we can begin thanking God not only for the healing of the spirit by deeper faith, but also for a more total healing according to the loving mind of God in his wisdom. In this life, in the providence of God, the increased healing is not always manifested in a bodily or psychical healing. Yet the very continued presence of the suffering is now a source of greater grace, happiness and spiritual health that will enhance the body and soul healing in the life to come.

Suffering in the Kingdom

We are always in need of deep trust in God in moments of suffering and humiliation and persecution inflicted upon us by others because of our Christian principles. Jesus pronounced a special blessing on such:

> Happy are you when people abuse you and persecute you and speak all kinds of calumny against you on my account. Rejoice and be glad, for your reward will be great in heaven; this is how they persecuted the prophets before you (Mt 5:11–12).

St. Paul also tells us that we will be called to suffer for the sake of Christ, "You are well aware, then, that anybody who tries to live in devotion to Christ is certain to be attacked" (2 Tm 3:12). Recognizing the difficulty of remaining loving toward those who inflict sufferings upon us, we must allow Jesus and his Spirit to bring us healing of our aggressive pride and selfishness.

As we lovingly and joyfully accept such adversities from others acting upon us, we begin to see them no longer as mere crosses, but as steps to a new transformation into Christ. We receive strength in deeper faith, hope and love to praise God for such happenings as we grow in greater gentleness and humility to God's loving presence and active concern for us. We may never like such sufferings, just as Jesus surely did not like his sufferings as he hung on the cross, but we can experience the blessings that flow from them when we abandon ourselves to let Jesus be Lord in such suffering occasions.

Filling Up the Sufferings of Christ

But there is still a higher motive for trusting God in our sufferings, especially those to be experienced in our own dying and death. Dietrich Bonhoeffer once wrote, "When Christ calls a man, he bids him come to die" (*The Cost of Discipleship*, p. 99). This is nothing but a paraphrase of Christ's invitation to his disciples to take up their crosses and follow him.

St. Peter teaches us the necessity of suffering, not because we have done wrong, but out of obedience to Christ's teachings (1 Pt 3:14–17). If Jesus warned his disciples to expect persecutions for his name's sake, then it is important to understand the relationship of our sufferings to Christ's sufferings and our communion with him, our head and risen-Lord, and with all members of the body of Christ.

St. Paul boldly declares, "It makes me happy to suffer for you, as I am suffering now, and in my own body to do what I can to make up all that has still to be undergone by Christ for the sake of his body, the Church" (Col 1:24). This text has always been difficult to understand in its fullest sense. In what way can Paul or we think Christ's sufferings are incomplete and that we can fill them up? We must reject any false understanding that would imply Christ's personal sufferings in his passion and death were insufficient for our redemption and that we would need to fill up the necessary sufferings.

Pope John Paul II in his apostolic letter on human suffering writes:

In Christ's cross, it is not only that the redemption is completed through the passion, but human suffering is itself redeemed. Christ...took to himself the whole evil of sin...when Christ achieved the redemption in his passion, he also raised human suffering to the level of the redemption. So it is that every human being in his or her suffering can become a sharer in the redemptive passion of Christ (No.19).

Members of the Body of Christ

If we keep in mind St. Paul's powerful analogy of the church as similar to a human body made up of many members and each member composed of cells that are interrelated with all other living cells of the entire body, then we may be able to understand a higher motive for accepting our sufferings joyfully.

We can become sharers in Christ's sufferings because Christ makes his passion and death through his resurrection available to us insofar as he has taken upon himself all our sins and sufferings through his sufferings on the cross. Through faith in Christ's passion we find redemption that is fresh and being applied to us through his ever-present dying-rising existence as head of his members in his body, the church. This is most perfectly symbolized in the celebration of the divine liturgy and climaxed in the reception of the Eucharist.

If we unfold the sufferings of Christ when we accept them in loving union with Christ-risen, we also to that degree witness and aid in bringing the resurrection of Christ to fulfillment in his body, the church. Communion in Christ's passion is the same as suffering to build up God's kingdom in this world. St. Paul writes, "Indeed, as the sufferings of Christ overflow to us, so, through Christ, does our consolation overflow" (2 Cor 1:5).

We should make our daily experience the prayer that St. Paul makes:

All I want is to know Christ and the power of his resurrection and to share his sufferings by reproducing the pattern of his death. That is the way I can hope to take my place in the resurrection of the dead (Phil 3:10–11).

Building the Body of Christ

As believers, therefore, our sufferings should never be independent of Christ's. As Christ once underwent his unique, individual sufferings, so now he endures or shares in our daily sufferings, for he will always now be one with the members of his body, the church. What we suffer in him and for him, out of love in his Spirit, he, as head, also suffers in the same Spirit that makes him one with his members.

Such human sufferings also have an eschatological effect. Our trials and tribulations, accepted in loving care and active responsibility to lessen the sufferings of other human beings, help to bring about the future of the fulfilled Christ, the total Christ. This includes the head in his members. But also, in the very moment of our accepting sufferings out of love for each other, we also share in a corporate raising of the entire body to a higher level of loving union with Christ the head.

Although we modern Christians know Jesus Christ alone is the mediator of the human race with the heavenly Father, yet we know through God's transforming grace what God has made of us in Christ Jesus. "It is all God's work. It was God who reconciled us to himself through Christ and gave us the work of handing on this reconciliation" (2 Cor 5:18). We are called into the awesome redemptive work by the merits of Jesus Christ to reconcile the sinful world to God. Jesus Christ has worked a purification in us through sufferings so we can already triumphantly cry out with St. Paul:

> I have been crucified with Christ, and I live now not with my own life but with the life of Christ who lives in me. The life I now live in this body I live in faith: faith in the Son of God who loved me and who sacrificed himself for my sake (Gal 2:19–20).

Christ's Suffering Presence to the World

Jesus shares his divine life with us, as he lives in us, as the vine is the life-giving source to the living branch. He is the head; we, in whom Jesus lives, make up his body. We are totally new in him and share in his power to intercede before the throne of the

Father. He "raised us up with him and gave us a place with him in heaven, in Christ Jesus" (Eph 2:6). We have been empowered to use his merits and his name, which is the only name whereby we shall be saved. It is his mediation, his intercession, that we share as we too groan in the Spirit of Jesus on behalf of a race of people that has forgotten God.

Like Abraham we beg, not on our own merits, but because of God's goodness made known through Jesus Christ, that men and women, cities and nations, the sick and suffering, the mentally confused and the disturbed be spared, and be healed, and be reconciled with God.

Incarnating the Good Samaritan

How can the suffering world be enlightened to the power of accepting their sufferings in and for Christ, unless they see him again teaching and acting out the parable of the Good Samaritan, the good neighbor, to the first person he meets as his brother or sister in need? How can others see the risen-Jesus, except by seeing him in us?

How can we pause and bring healing love to the suffering whom we meet, unless we have learned to suffer meaningfully in Christ, the crucified risen-Lord? Only then can we become the good Samaritan to those who suffer in wasted pain by being the one who shows active compassion by making a gift of ourselves because, humbly, by God's grace, we have learned that the course of suffering leads to glory. Death to selfishness is to share in Christ's resurrection in this present moment by doing whatever we do to the least of our brothers and sisters and knowing we *really* do these things to Christ!

CHAPTER 8

Trust in the Dark Night

John Tauler, a 14th–century Rhenish mystic and Dominican theologian, prayed for eight years that God would send him a person who would be able to point out to him the true way to perfection. One day while he was in prayer Tauler felt this desire come over him very strongly. He heard a voice from within telling him to go to the steps of the church, and there he would meet such a teacher.

Tauler found on the steps of the church a beggar in rags, with feet bare, wounded and caked with mud. He greeted the beggar with the words: "May God give you a good day." The beggar answered: "I do not remember ever having had a bad day." Tauler asked the beggar to explain how it was that he never had a bad day, never had been anything but happy. The beggar answered:

> You wished me a good day, and I answered that I cannot recall having ever spent a bad day. For, when famishing with hunger, I praise God equally; when I am in want, when I am rebuffed and despised, I still praise God; and, consequently, I know not what it is to have a bad day. You next wished me a good and happy life, and I replied that I have never been otherwise than happy. That is perfectly true. For I have learned how to live with God, and I am convinced that whatever He does must necessarily be very good. Hence, everything which I receive from God, or which He permits that I receive from others, prosperity or adversity, sweet or bitter, I regard as a particular favor, and I accept it with joy from His hand. Besides, it is my first resolution never to attach myself to anything but the will of God alone. I have so merged my own will in His that whatsoever He wills, I will also. Therefore, I have been always happy.

The beggar had given all for All and had found the secret of happiness. It consisted in perfect childlike abandonment to the

129

.venly Father's will in all circumstances of life and joining such
.rrender to profound humility. This is the shortest road to God.

Goal of All Human Striving

We have pointed out already in various ways that the constant teaching in Christian spirituality is that there can be no
transformation into loving union with the Blessed Trinity, dwelling within the baptized Christian, without the necessary purification of the heart of all self-centeredness, in order to "put on"
completely the mind of Christ.

The goal of Jesus on this earth was always, in each event, to
return the Father's love for him by obeying perfectly, in all
details, the will of the Father. Jesus is more than an extrinsic
pattern of how we can return God's perfect love by doing always
the Father's will. He, as the risen-Lord who lives within us, and by
his Spirit (we know this with absolute knowledge given by the
Spirit), becomes the Way to return our filial love with praise,
gratitude and trust as we live in intimate union with him.

In union with Jesus we can together live our yes toward the
same heavenly Father. We can say, "Our Father, hallowed be thy
name, thy kingdom come, thy will be done on earth as it is in
heaven." It is Jesus living in us, guiding our daily lives, as we live
in, through and with him the Father's plan of infinite Love,
Wisdom and Power.

Yet how many Christians are ready to enter into the various
stages of purification in order to attain the state of mystical
oneness with Jesus Christ? How many, even among so-called
dedicated Christians, are ready to surrender completely to the
infusion of the Holy Spirit's faith, hope and love, to move into
the dark nights of deeper purification?

Our Active Purification

As we have already pointed out in the preceding chapter on
trusting in God at all times, especially in trials and sufferings, God
is actively involved in lovingly purifying our hearts. The only
obstacle in us that impedes the continuous inflow of God's
infinite love into our spirit comes from the wall of self-centeredness. This can be fully removed only through complete abandon-

ment to God's providential working in the events of moment. We are called by God's Spirit, as Jesus was, to enter i. the desert of our hearts and do the battle that will integra. ourselves into a oneness of our true self in intimate union with Jesus, and a oneness in will to do always the holy will of "our Father."

This is the teaching of St. Paul directed to the Thessalonians:

> May the God of peace make you perfect and holy; and may you all be kept safe and blameless, spirit, soul and body, for the coming of our Lord Jesus Christ. God has called you and he will not fail you (1 Thes 5:23).

The test of how integrated we have become in our true selves in oneness with Jesus is also given by St. Paul:

> Be happy at all times; pray constantly; and for all things give thanks to God, because this is what God expects you to do in Christ Jesus.
>
> Never try to suppress the Spirit or treat the gift of prophecy with contempt; think before you do anything — hold on to what is good and *avoid every* form of *evil* (1 Thes 5:16–22).

We are to be active in attaining such docility to the movements of the Holy Spirit. We are searching, with God's grace and indwelling presence, to find our true self in a loving union with the Trinity as we choose to participate in God's shared nature. But this demands an inner vigilance over the egotistic tendencies in our relationships with God, neighbor and the world around us.

There is so much more of us to come into being if only we have the courage to enter into the interior battle. God is calling us constantly to a process of his loving activities, to let go of the controlled activity we have been exercising in our daily life, especially seen mirrored forth in the type of prayer in which we may find ourselves locked. Some of us stand at the edge of the barren desert. Will we come to trust in God's providential and loving care for us by seeking to move away from our bias toward self and surrender in the darkness that awaits us to whatever God, our loving Father, wills for us?

the total abandonment of our will to God's will, when used by the Spirit's gifts of faith, hope and love, is the full and perfect living of our personal relationship to God in the experience of Christ's own divine peace penetrating every level of our being.

Trust can never be developed merely by praying for this gift. It is acquired along with deeper faith, hope and love in the "battle." It is in our life-situations that we meet God's will for us and learn to surrender actively to his loving presence in any given moment.

We have already discovered how in the past events of our life certain trials and deprivations became occasions for the development of trust in God's love for us and in his wisdom to bring about greater purity of heart. At times such deprivations are felt in the loss of a parent, spouse or dear friend through death. Such persons have been of great help to us, but now we need to trust in God, who above all other loves in our life is working for our sanctification, even in what appeared to be a great loss.

Perhaps the gifts and resources we once possessed and exercised freely now have diminished or even have been taken away from us. These might be health, time for leisure, intellectual talents. Such a loss can often lead to greater trust in cases of our inability to serve others through God's gifts to us. What sadness can cover our horizon when we begin to experience failures in works of zeal done for God's glory! St. Bernard felt his involvement in preaching the second crusade was all for nought, yet he learned to trust in God's presence in his failure since the pope had expressly commanded him to preach it.

As we become older and the dreams of earlier years perhaps turn sour, we need great trust in such disappointments and great wisdom from the Spirit of God to find God's will operating in all. We learn to abandon ourselves to God's presence and to seek to discover higher motives by which we can measure achievements and true success in God's eyes.

We trust that God is working with perfect love in any negativity, especially in seeing the lack of success in our spiritual life of prayer and the uprooting of selfishness with a greater love in service toward others. On this level of trials that come to us in

our specific relationship with God, we find interior te
and aridity combined often with desolations that touch .
our spiritual, but also psychic and sense levels.

For a sensitive Christian temptations will take on propor
of great suffering, depending on the degree of experienced unr
with God through ever-increasing faith, hope and love. Suc
temptations make the fervent Christian think he or she is in
danger of losing the Lord. God becomes even more present to
such a suffering Christian, whose pride is broken down in the
urgency to call upon the Lord as his or her sole strength in
such temptations.

Aridity, and even a sense of depression and desolation, can
last for a long time. Yet the key in bearing such trials depends on
our detachment from all affections for earthly creatures, even
spiritual consolations. Spiritual pride, and even spiritual glut-
tony, are attacked and conquered by such trials.

St. Francis de Sales wisely gives us the proper way for a
Christian to bear all temptations, aridities, aversions and repug-
nances, especially in prayer:

> If consolations are offered,
> receive them with gratitude;
> If they are refused,
> desire them not,
> but try to keep your heart ready
> to welcome whatsoever Providence may send,
> and as far as possible,
> with satisfaction....
> You must have a strong resolution
> never to give up prayer,
> no matter what difficulties
> you may encounter in that holy exercise.
> And you must never apply yourself to it,
> preoccupied with a longing
> to be consoled and favored....
> Provided we always accommodate our wills
> to the will of his Divine Majesty,
> remaining in an attitude
> of simple expectation
> and in a disposition

_ceive lovingly
atever Providence may ordain,
vhether in our prayer,
or outside of it,
he will see to it that
everything is made conducive
to our profit
and pleasing in his sight *(Treatise on the Love of God)*.

Our Weaknesses Become Our Strength

True children of God realize in life's circumstances that we have no strength of our own. In all moments we are to confess our weaknesses to do good by our own efforts. We know with St. Paul that all our strength is to be found in Christ. Our very weakness, when recognized, can become our strength as we lovingly surrender to God in all things. Any trials that come to us must be accepted joyfully as we place our hope in our weaknesses in God.

St. Paul provides us with the proper, humble attitude:

So I shall be very happy to make my weaknesses my special boast so that the power of Christ may stay over me, and that is why I am quite content with my weaknesses, and with insults, hardships, persecutions, and the agonies I go through for Christ's sake. For it is when I am weak that I am strong (2 Cor 12:9–10).

The fruit that our heavenly Father wishes us to bring forth is a constant, loving submission and obedience to his commands and wishes. To believe that the Father truly loves us and does all things out of love is the basis for our childlike surrender.

No present moment of our life, whatever it may bring us — sorrows, joys, sickness or bubbling health — is ever judged as banal, unpleasant, or even simply exciting and beautiful. The poetry in the heart of a person who has been converted and has become a child of God allows him or her to see much more of God in each event than most others do. God saturates this "now" moment with his personal presence, with the gift of himself to us. This makes everything everywhere a sacred place for God to surprise us with his love, which can never be limited to any special place or time or circumstance.

Call to Contemplation

I would like to focus upon the higher levels of prayer with the accompanying purifications necessary if we are to continue into more intimate union with the Trinity. We have pointed out that the true test of our union with the Divine consists in the total surrender of our will to the will of God. To do God's will through perfect obedience is the true test of how great our love is for God who has given us all things in his Son, Jesus Christ, through his Spirit of love.

We are to live such a union in each moment of our life by exercising the Spirit's gifts of faith, hope and love. Such a state of abandonment to the Father's will is a blending of faith, hope and love in one single act that unites us to God and all his activities. As we advance toward such union of *being* one with Christ through the Father's Spirit of love, we find our prayer-life depending on greater trust in God's loving presence and activities working within us and all around us.

Trials and struggles to believe in God's perfect, self-emptying love for us find their greatest intensity in our intimate, spiritual relationship with God, Father, Son and Holy Spirit, in the level of prayer. When exterior trials and sufferings hit us in our daily living, we can more easily divert our attention to persons and things around us. But after we have prayed with oral and discursive meditation in which our faith, hope and love have grown slowly over months and years of using our imagination, memory, understanding and will to become aware of God's presence to us, God calls us to an interior state of deep purification.

As our act of faith in God's presence within us grows, the Spirit of the risen-Jesus steadily moves us away from centering upon our activities in prayer and brings us into a state of *being*. It is in such prayer without words and images, and our own actively directing the dialogue with God, that we begin to see the boundaries dissolve between our prayer-life and our "normal" activities.

We begin to yield with greater susceptibility to Christ's loving presence. Our aggressive activity, both in prayer and in daily actions, takes on a gentleness and docility to the indwelling presence of the Trinity, both within us and within all of creation around us. Everything seems to shout out that God is here! This place indeed is holy! There is a letting go of our power and a new sensitivity, a new listening to God's presence and loving activity around us. We seem to be living on a new plateau of awareness of God's presence and his working in our life.

At first this more contemplative mode of praying fills us with excitement and great feeling. We have received from God's Spirit a burst of spiritual energy that operates intensely in the time of our formal prayer and throughout the day, but on a lesser "feeling" way. There is a growing sense of unity with God and with the rest of creation. Anxieties are quickly replaced by a childlike trust in the Father. The name of Jesus is constantly on our lips and in our heart.

Signs of Contemplative Prayer

St. John of the Cross has masterfully presented signs that indicate that an individual is being led by the Holy Spirit through deeper faith, hope and love from discursive meditation to a state of contemplative prayer. The first indication of being called into contemplative prayer is the realization that we can no longer habitually meditate as before, with the stress placed on our activities. Dryness only comes when we seek to concentrate with our imagination, intellect, emotions and will upon mental images and words.

The second sign is that we discover no desire to fix the imagination upon perceptual images and words moving in a logic from our intellect to our will. The third leads us to a desire to remain simply aware of God's loving presence. The name of Jesus brings us into his risen presence. He was dead, and now he is alive through the Spirit's increased faith, hope and love.

We realize that this mode of contemplative prayer does not begin suddenly, but is a result of long preparation on our part and much hard work to reach a simple look of faith upon the indwelling Lord.

The Dark Nights

It helps us to a greater understanding of trust and childlike abandonment if we study the purifications that come with such intensity of the prayer of faith, hope and love. Since such prayer can no longer be separated from our daily life, because the stronger in our formal prayer we are in surrendering in trust to whatever God-Trinity wishes to do to us, the stronger, also, will be our trust in the events of our daily life. We will discover that as we pray so we live; as we are purified in contemplative prayer, so we are purified in the very human situations of daily living.

After receiving so much in meditation over years of fidelity in our disciplined prayer time, alone with the Alone, by way of ideas, insights, affective feelings of God's loving presence in our formal prayer, we feel that God is calling us to tear down the scaffolding that we built to reach God. God's presence as an inner light or illumination turns to an inner darkness. Affections dry up in prayer, leaving only stark aridity with the inner desert so huge and we seemingly so lost.

With the Bride in the Song of Songs we now complain: "I sought him whom my heart loves. I sought but did not find him" (Sg 3:1). God purifies our attachment to his gifts, as he prunes us from all sensible delights that up until now, perhaps, we used as the test of our oneness with Christ. He invites us to enter into various aspects of a new way of knowing and possessing him, which St. John of the Cross calls the Night. John's teaching is in harmony with the doctrine of such earlier mystics as Origen, St. Gregory of Nyssa, Pseudo-Dionysius, Meister Eckhart and John Tauler.

St. John of the Cross is the recognized master of how we are to trust in God's providential love and caring in his teaching on the two types of Night, or purifications in deeper prayer. These are the Night of the senses and the Night of the spirit. Each purification has two aspects: one active, with the ascetical stress on the individual's vigilant battling to uproot inordinate, passionate attachments; and one mystical, with the stress on God's activity and, hence, passivity, or active receptivity, on the part of the individual Christian contemplative.

Dark Night of the Senses

In order to develop purity of heart we are called to be actively involved in the ascetical practices, which can never become ends in themselves, but always necessary means, if we are to continue on our journey to our heavenly Father. On the negative side, such ascetical practices of vigilance over our "heart" are aimed toward the uprooting of any inordinate, passionate (self-centered) desires that constitute obstacles to greater union with Christ.

We could express St. John's teaching of this negative side in terms of the necessity to rid ourself of any compulsive behavior, of any "thoughtless" self-indulgence in thought, word or deed. Any such pre-conditioned actions or thoughts that bind us in a slavery to senses or internal faculties of emotions, imagination, memory, intellect or will, take us away from our being centered in loving obedience upon God alone. To become God-conscious, we need to place more and more of our life in all of its activities under God's will.

Control of our sensual (rooted in the senses) and psychic and spiritual faculties will aid us in being centered upon God. Fragmentation toward every desire impedes inner attention and oneness with God and must be corrected by inner vigilance. This is the prime work of the active Night of the senses; that is, the withdrawal of deliberate desire from the objects of inordinate sense satisfaction by creating a greater desire for God and union with him. Such going against a nature that has been pre-conditioned to act without reference to God's holy will in every thought, word and deed will always bring about a certain suffering. And above all, there is suffering involved in a special trusting in God in the trials undergone to be more in conformity with God's will. But always the Christian hope lies in a necessary therapy of such suffering leading to greater life in Christ. "Unless a wheat grain falls on the ground and dies, it remains only a grain; but if it dies, it yields a rich harvest" (Jn 12:24).

God expects us to be attentive and to uproot any sinful attachments to sense pleasures; he expects us to develop the Christian virtues, which will allow us to put on the mind of Christ. He himself calls us to enter into his special activities of purifying us from excessive self-centeredness through sense satisfaction. It is on this level of freely and joyfully surrendering to God's purifying hand that will determine whether or not we will make any progress in contemplative prayer.

Signs of the Night of the Senses

God has created all human beings that we may all come into a mystical oneness with his Son, Jesus Christ, and in that oneness share, through the Spirit of the risen-Jesus, oneness with the Father. God, therefore, wishes to lead all of us from the exercise of our controlled use in prayer of our imagination, memory, understanding and will. The reason God so purifies us away from our control is that he cannot break through on the spiritual level as long as *we* are directing the prayerful dialogue. This usually hardens after years of such discursive prayer into a monologue where we are the main attraction, the doer, but not the loving listener.

God begins his process of purifying us of our illusory absorption in ourselves as though we were the center of all reality by throwing us into extreme aridity in prayer and throughout our waking hours. We trust in God's loving acts of purification, which are means to allow us a greater conscious sharing in his own divine life. St. John of the Cross expresses this divine motive well:

> As I said, when God sees that they have grown a little, he weans them from the sweet breast so that they might be strengthened, lays aside their swaddling bands and puts them down from his arms that they may grow accustomed to walking by themselves. This change is a surprise to them because everything seems to be functioning in reverse (*The Dark Night of the Soul* I:8,3).

God purifies us not merely during our prayer time but throughout the day's activities. The signs are clear that God is working to lead us beyond the trammeling of our sense attachments to creatures to a complete trust and abandonment to his holy will. The first sign, according to St. John of the Cross, that God is actively working upon us, is that we find no consolation or satisfaction from the things of God such as our own devotions, the Mass, our prayer and our attempts at recollection throughout the day, or from any other of God's creatures (*Night* I:9,2).

The second sign of such purification taking place is that we think we are not serving God, but rather that we are turning away from God since we do not have a taste for the things of God (*Night* I:9,3).

The third sign is the powerlessness we experience to return to meditation and carry on some meaningful dialogue with God. God is not communicating himself through the senses and the interior faculties as before on a lower level of prayer. He wishes to lead us to his self-communication through our spirit and his Spirit, who bear united witness that we are truly God's children.

Rules for Survival in the Night

These rules can also, with some adaptation, be used for the purifications God sends us, or allows to happen to us, in the context of our living situation as well as in times of formal prayer.

1. Perseverance in our aridity, when we have discerned humbly before God that such is not a result of our own tepidity. Increase the search for God alone. Focus all desire on serving him alone. Intensify vigilance so that no inordinate desire for consolations may draw us away from the Divine Physician.

2. Be ready to accept willingly, even with joy, the purifications that come to us in forms other than excessive aridity in prayer. These will show up in our daily encounters with those closest to us. Accept with peace and childlike trust in God's loving care for us our inability to cope with the nitty-gritty problems of daily life.

3. Transform such humiliations and ineffectiveness on our part into greater reverence and humility before God in our prayer time and in our recollection throughout the day.

4. Use the purifications sent us in interpersonal relationships as a humbling means to move from an *animus* judgmental attitude to an *anima* gentleness. Love others with the love of Christ, with a purer heart and greater desire to show them mercy and loving service.

5. Increase our desire to remain habitually present to God as our sole strength and source of love throughout the active hours of our day.

6. St. John of the Cross summarizes what our attitude sh.
in the purification of the senses. We are being challeng
accept this stage of our journey in faith with great genero
believing with Jeremiah: "You have disciplined me,
accepted the discipline" (Jer 31:18; *Night* I:12,3).

How Long the Night?

It is difficult to estimate the amount of time God permits such
a state of purification. We can only trust in God's love and
wisdom. Those who are weak, he may keep in this night for a long
time with a purification less intense. This might continue over
their whole life, interrupted by God's consoling presence to
strengthen them in their journey. For those who have greater
strength for suffering (and God does give his graces differently to
each person), God purges more intensely and quickly. We can see
how God coordinates such purification in a person's position in
life, responsibilities to others and psychic equilibrium with what
he does directly in time of formal prayer.

Glory in the Cross of Jesus Christ

We learn in such purifications to trust in the Father's infinite
love and wisdom. He knows all about us, especially the deeper
levels of our false ego-centered self, our hidden addictions in our
inherited bias toward self, our collective-unconscious, whose
depths of selfishness we ourselves are not even aware of to a
great degree. In God's loving providence, we learn to trust in such
sufferings. We learn actively to respond in faith to St. Paul's
teaching:

> And if we are children we are heirs as well: heirs of God
> and coheirs with Christ, sharing his sufferings so as to
> share his glory.
> I think that what we suffer in this life can never be
> compared to the glory, as yet unrevealed, which is wait-
> ing for us (Rom 8:17–18).

Behind every cross, adversity, trial or suffering in our physical, mental and spiritual life, every seeming death-dealing situation experienced in our family, work or social life, there is the

Father working through his Son and Holy Spirit. He
es for each of us the crosses that will be most effective in
ing us of our unknown, hidden areas of self-centeredness and
k of true agapic love.

Dark Night of the Spirit

Perhaps for most Christians this is an area of extreme suffering that will remain unknown to them in this life. Yet heaven
cannot be possible as a mystical oneness, comparable only in kind
to a mystical marriage, with Christ Jesus, who opens to us the
infinite love of the Father through their mutual loving Spirit,
unless in the life to come we eventually submit willingly to the
necessary therapy known as purgatory.

For those more advanced and courageous, who live on this
earth in deeper faith, hope and love, there is a final purification,
one that brings us into deepest union with Christ in the paschal
mystery. This is what St. John of the Cross calls the dark night of
the spirit. It is the greatest, most complete and thorough of all
purifications experienced in this life. It corrects all the damage
done by original and personal sin. It restores us to the lost state of
innocence experienced by our first parents before the fall.

The end and aim of our human life, as we have been pointing
out in this chapter, is mystical union with God in our immediate
oneness with Christ, our Bridegroom, who has died for each of us
in order that we might share in the union he enjoys with the
Father through the Holy Spirit. This cannot come about by our
efforts or any efforts on our human level of activity. Of ourself, we
have nothing that is by our nature oriented to this union with
God, Trinity, through Jesus Christ.

The need of the dark night of the spirit, the need of identifica-
tion with Jesus in his radical poverty of spirit, his total self-
emptying, is the highest point before transformation and union
take place in mystical prayer. It is the purification that brings
about our human reintegration into the triune, divine life by our
intimate union with Jesus-Lord.

We must surrender to God's complete control on all levels of
our being, both of the senses and in our rational self-directing. We
enter into a void, an emptiness of all that may impede us from

being totally surrendered to God's Spirit of love. There is no longer a clinging to any human knowledge derived by our own reasoning. The words of the prophet Isaiah are especially meaningful:

> Let anyone who fears Yahweh among you
> listen to the voice of his servant!
> Whoever walks in darkness,
> and has no light shining for him,
> let him trust in the name of Yahweh,
> let him lean on his God (Is 50:10).

Transformation Into Christ

We can be transformed and united with the triune-God. We can become God by participation in his divine nature only if we let go of everything, so that God can take complete possession of us and refashion us. This is the work the Father, in the person of his Son, and through the Holy Spirit, accomplishes in us through the radical purification process that is the dark night of the spirit. It is the full meaning of the power and wisdom of the cross in identifying us with our Head and Bridegroom in his resurrectional life, which becomes our resurrectional life, precisely because it is his, the Life of him who is our life.

We return to our true state, to a consciousness of being *in Christ* and, through love, to live now according to that dignity in all of our human relationships. Yet this transformation is never a static condition; it is a dynamic process of continued purification and a dying to selfishness with a continued rising to a more intense conscious relationship to God. This is a state of harmony that, when it is attained, brings us peace and inner tranquility. This is in proportion to the degree that we cut out of our lives any inordinate desires except the one great and passionate desire to love God more intensely and become more united in Christ by the transforming union with him.

Love is the consuming fire that now burns in the heart of the contemplative Christian. No mystic has better captured this state

transforming union in love through sufferings than St. John of
the Cross:

> O living flame of love
> That tenderly wounds my soul
> In its deepest center!
> Now you are not oppressive,
> Now Consummate! if it be Your will:
> Tear through the veil of this sweet encounter!
>
> O sweet cautery,
> O delightful wound!
> O gentle hand! of delicate touch
> That tastes of eternal life
> And pays every debt!
> In killing, You changed death to life.
>
> O lamps of fire!
> In whose splendors
> The deep caverns of feeling,
> Once obscure and blind,
> Now give forth, so rarely,
> So exquisitely,
> Both warmth and light to their Beloved.
>
> How gently and lovingly
> You wake in my heart,
> Where in Your sweet breathing,
> Filled with good and glory,
> How tenderly You swell my heart with love
> (*The Living Flame of Love*, pp. 578–79).

This is the deepest meaning and fruitfulness of the dark night
of the spirit; it is the Father's purifying activity of love through
the infusion of his divine light and love, which, in the measure it
destroys in us all that is opposed to God's light and love, is a form
of infused contemplation that can only be called painful.

Forms of Suffering That Lead to Union

St. John of the Cross, again, describes the goal of such
sufferings that come to us in the dark night of the spirit.

This Dark Night, then, is an inflow of God into the soul which purges it of its "habitual" ignorances and imperfections, natural and spiritual, and which contemplatives call Infused Contemplation. Through this contemplation, God teaches the soul secretly and instructs it in the perfection of love without its doing anything nor understanding how this happens (*The Dark Night* II, 8, 4).

We must keep in mind that greater trust is developed in this state of prayer and union with Christ than in any earlier level of prayer. Now prayer and a life of action become more a united state of *being* in trustful abandonment to Jesus Christ-risen to let him speak his word in every circumstance of our human life as we surrender to let his will be done in us.

The sufferings endured through the Father's purifying light and love can assume many forms, different for each person. We should read the various descriptions of sufferings that such mystics as St. John of the Cross and St. Teresa of Avila experienced as symbols, and not as concrete sufferings that all of us must suffer in the identical form they experienced them.

It is important to keep our eyes fixed on the degree of trust and abandonment we develop under the Spirit of the risen-Lord as we undergo specific sufferings that come to us through the providential wisdom of God, who knows how to purify us in order to lead us into the transforming union with his Divine Son.

Some people enter into a severe suffering through the seeming loss of the Divine Presence. Others experience the agony of their own sinful unworthiness seen in the blazing light of God's holiness and goodness to them. Only the individual can understand the particular suffering he or she is undergoing. But the results are always the same: The purifications lead the individual to a total self-emptying, a total abandonment to the infinite, loving mercy of the Father, who seeks to transform his child into his own splendor and beauty, through the very reality of the depth of the humiliations suffered.

Another type of suffering common to such children of God, who begin to learn how to trust God in his exercise of purifying love, is the spiritual distaste for God and the things of God. This always brings with it a sense of guilt that perhaps the individual

...ay turned away from God in selfishness. Thus, the person
...es and becomes ever more distrustful in his or her power to
...roach God worthily.

...ufferings in the Active Life

Religious and lay persons who lead very active lives of service
to others should keep in mind that the actual style of life is not the
essence of the dark night of the spirit. What counts is our
readiness, both in personal prayer before God and in the activities
performed in loving service to those around us, to seek God's will
in loving trust. God may work to purify us through ill-health,
difficulties and clashes arising through differences of tempera-
ment, misunderstandings and a dangerous preoccupation to "succeed" in a given apostolate. We learn in such seeming failures to
surrender to God's purifying love.

We can be certain that there is one suffering God does not
wish us to accept, and that is to entertain the slightest doubt or
uncertainty about his everlasting love for us. Thus we can keep
our eyes clearly on the goal of such purifications and the resulting
transforming union with Jesus Christ as we surrender in deepen-
ing trust to the Father's burning love for us to share his triune life
through the union of love we enjoy now as a constant state of
being one in Jesus.

The test of our trusting in God's providential care in such
sufferings has to be measured always by our readiness to enter into
complete self-emptying in order always to allow God's purifying
love to lead us. Through darkness into the light of a flaming,
transforming love and union with Jesus Christ we are united
through our mystical oneness with him to be one through him
with the Father and his Holy Spirit.

As we cry out for the face of God to appear in our darkness of
the spirit, the Father does hear us and brings us into a sharing with
the risen-Lord, Jesus, to whom the Father has given charge
through his Holy Spirit to lift us up, even now, to share in eternal
life.

We can see the sufferings in the dark night of the spirit in
broad terms of our journey from baptism, when we first pledged
ourselves to give up the wiles of the Prince of Darkness in order to

follow the light of Christ, the Savior, to the climax in the eucharistic union. This gives us a oneness with the risen-Jesus through the living out of our own unique sacrifice of bearing the crosses and suffering to fill up the sufferings in the body of Christ, which leads to a sharing also in his glorious, resurrectional life in complete oneness with the Lord of the universe.

St. John of the Cross summarizes the fruit of the sufferings we are asked to endure in the dark night of the spirit:

> This state of a relatively perfect love of God consists in the total transformation of our will into the Will of God, in such wise that henceforth there is nothing in our will which is contrary to the Father's Will; in all and through all we are moved...solely by the Will of the Father, so that out of two wills is formed one will, the Will of God which is also our will (*Ascent to Mount Carmel* I, 2, 2–3).

This, after all, is the promise of Jesus Christ given to his disciples before he went to his dark night of the spirit on the cross:

> Anybody who receives my commandments and keeps them
> will be one who loves me;
> and anybody who loves me will be loved by my Father,
> and I shall love him and show myself to him....
> If anyone loves me he will keep my word,
> and my Father will love him,
> and we shall come to him
> and make our home with him....
> (and) the Advocate, the Holy Spirit,
> whom the Father will send in my name,
> will teach you everything and remind you of all I have said to you (Jn 14:21–26).

An Unending Process of Continued Growth

Trusting in God's transforming power in all events never reaches a static end of completion. A person who has been given new eyes of deeper faith, hope and love through purifying sufferings of the dark night of the spirit, learns to see the transfiguring power of the triune community of love working in the world. The person has discovered the paradoxical reality of death through sufferings that transform him or her through surrendering trust and love into a greater union with Jesus Christ.

An inner urge burns within the individual always to reach greater degrees of union with Christ. He or she ardently moves forward in each event to embrace fully the presence of God as love in that moment. Contemplatives purified by the dark night of the spirit look at the same events as do other persons, but they see deeper inside and touch the loving presence of God. They surrender actively to go with that light and never step out into the darkness of self-centeredness. They learn to live in "luminous darkness," which unveils the loving, caring activities of the Father in his Son, Jesus Christ, through their mutual Spirit of Love.

Even though God is the Rock — firm, stable and immovable — yet, for contemplatives who abandon themselves to God's loving Providence, God is always in movement. He fills all things, yet he transcends everything. He is immaterial, and yet he pervades all matter. He is eternal Light, yet he comes to such prayerful Christians in the very darkness of the night of the spirit. He has no mouth to speak, yet he utters his Word within them and from inside each event. He has no hand to grasp his earthly children and guide them, yet they learn that God does touch them with his divine hand and raises them up in the light to gaze on his loving face. That divine hand gives an assurance, a power and a certainty that nothing can take away.

Such Christian contemplatives enter into a solidarity with the saints and angels, with the living members of the body of Christ, the church. They are one with the suffering world, with those who lie in darkness and have not yet seen the light. They burn actively to bring them into the light. They are humble and feel privileged to wash the feet of their brothers and sisters, since they have experienced Christ in their union with him, who "emptied himself...even to accepting death, death on a cross" (Phil 2:7–8).

Transforming Power of Surrendering Trust

To the degree that we Christians surrender ourselves freely to the leadership of Jesus Christ through the mystical oneness we enjoy with him and in him, to that degree we can say we are Christians, living members of his body. We will know experientially that we live in his light by the gentle love we have toward each person whom we meet in each moment.

Thus we will be led from moment to moment into greater light as we see, by increased faith, hope and love, God's loving presence in all events. Complete abandonment and childlike trust are the Holy Spirit's gifts to those who are ready to die to their false selves and begin to live in the truth of the new creatures that they are and have always been in the eyes of the heavenly Father.

Jesus, I Trust in You!

Permit me to end this book on trust in Jesus, who lives within us and transforms us in each moment of life into his image, by quoting these words of J. P. de Caussade, S.J.:

> O my God, when will it please you to give me the grace of remaining habitually in that union of my will with Your adorable will, in which, without our saying anything, all is said, and in which we do everything by letting You act. In this perfect union of wills, we perform immense tasks because we work more in conformity with Your good pleasure; and yet we are dispensed from all toil because we place the care of everything in Your hands, and think of nothing but of reposing completely in You, a delightful state, which even in the absence of all feelings of faith, gives the soul an interior and altogether spiritual relish. Let me say, then, unceasingly through the habitual disposition of my heart, "Fiat!" Yes, my God, yes, everything that You please. May Your holy desires be fulfilled in everything. I give up my own, which are blind, perverse and corrupted by that miserable self-love which is the mortal enemy of Your grace and pure love, of Your glory, and my own sanctification (*Self-Abandonment to Divine Providence*, p. 449).